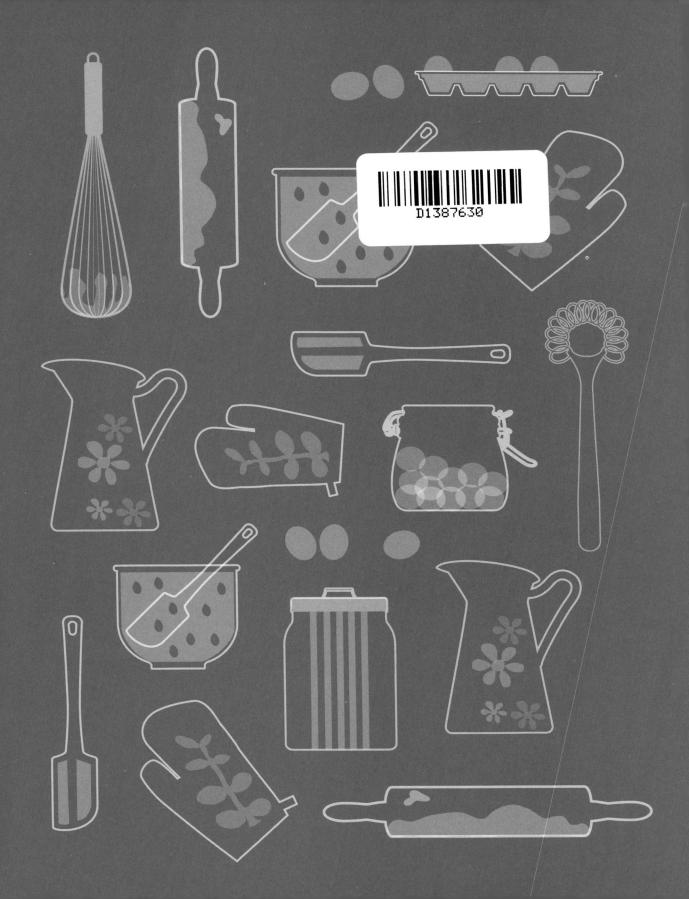

D1387630

National Trust

— COMPLETE —

Country
Cookbook

Laura Mason

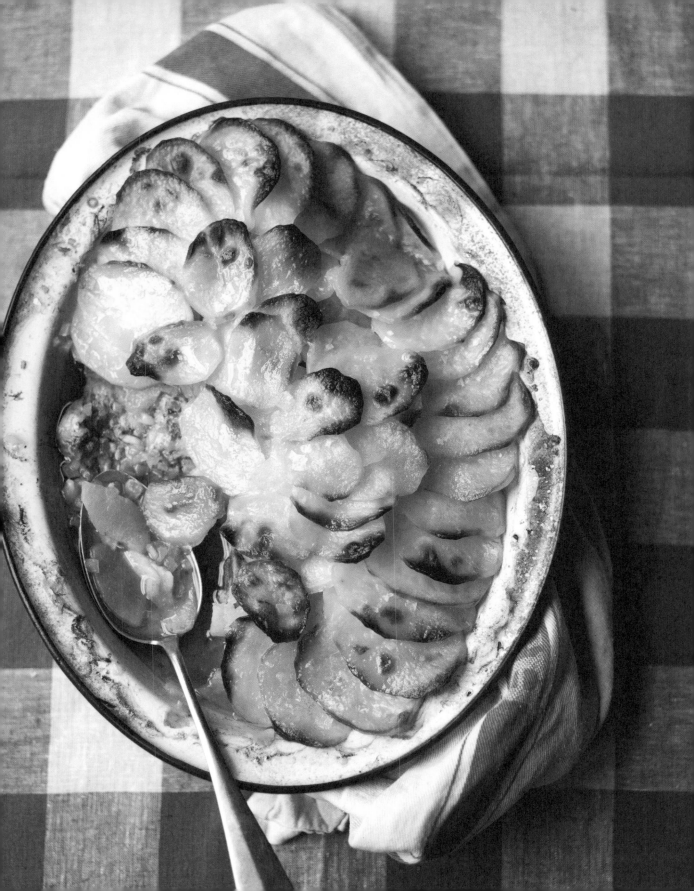

National Trust
— COMPLETE —
Country
Cookbook

Laura Mason

National Trust

First published in the United Kingdom in 2005 as *Farmhouse Cookery* by
The National Trust (Enterprises) Ltd, then revised in 2009.

This edition first published in 2012 by
National Trust Books
10 Southcombe Street
London W14 0RA
An imprint of Anova Books Ltd

ISBN: 9781907892400

A CIP catalogue record for this book is available from the British Library.

20 19 18 17 16 15 14 13 12
10 9 8 7 6 5 4 3 2 1

Printed and bound by Craft Print International Ltd, Singapore
Reproduction by Mission Productions Ltd, Hong Kong

Produced by SP Creative Design
Editor: Heather Thomas
Designer: Rolando Ugolini
Food photography: Tara Fisher
Home economist: Jane Suthering
Food styling: Wei Tang

Acknowledgements
All the recipes are © Laura Mason except the following:
Sarah Edington: pages 26, 38, 54, 108, 134, 150, 186, 220, 248, 264, 276
Jane Pettigrew: pages 184, 190, 204

Some of the recipes have previously appeared in the following National Trust titles:
Good Old-fashioned Pies and Stews; *Good Old-fashioned Roasts*; *The National Trust Complete Traditional Recipe Book*; *Traditional Teatime Recipes*.

Contents

Introduction

This book celebrates two things: the tradition of country cookery, and the link between the landscape and food, especially as it is experienced through food produced by the tenants of National Trust properties. The Trust is far more than aristocratic houses; it manages farmland scattered across England, Wales and Northern Ireland. The model farm at Wimpole in East Anglia, the little fields of the Cornish coast, the deer parks of the Welsh Marches, the mountains of Snowdonia and the fells of the Lake District all have one thing in common – they have been shaped over the centuries by food production.

Beautiful landscapes may appear to be eternal combinations of grass, rock and water, but much of their charm comes from precise systems of land use. The seemingly perfect vernacular buildings that are characteristic of such landscapes – great barns, isolated farmsteads, and pleasingly composed hamlets or villages – are products of working on a human scale within the constraints of local materials. Food, either as raw ingredients or in particular recipes, could equally be seen as an expression of locality, of local taste working with available materials.

Many of the cookery traditions of the countryside were gradually eroded by urbanisation in the nineteenth century, and then further diluted by the expediencies of rationing during World War II and the modern phenomenon of supermarkets. However, in spite of this, many people are still keeping country cookery and baking traditions alive, some regularly cooking recipes that have been used by their families or in their region for generations, while others are developing new ideas within the constraints of what their land produces. Some of their recipes and ideas appear in this book, which features a balance of traditional 'good plain cooking' and rich, well-seasoned dishes, often rooted in a particular region and focusing on local products. Tradition changes subtly, and some much-loved and symbolic foods, such as fruit cakes, have little to do with our landscapes, yet they preserve memories

of distant fashions and novelties in an edible form, which has altered gradually over time. The rhythms of rural life influenced country meals and dishes and led to slow-cooked, hearty stews and hotpots, and the rituals of baking bread, plain and fancy cakes, and pies.

The meals and dishes eaten in the countryside had their own internal logic. For example, farmers rose between five and six and had a cup of tea and a bite to eat before the first milking. After two or three hours, they adjourned for a more substantial breakfast of porridge or bacon, eggs and toast or teacakes. The day's agenda was set by the season, but it always involved routine work, and was punctuated by dinner (eaten at lunchtime), which was the biggest meal. Everyday dinners required filling, warming dishes, such as stews and hotpots, which looked after themselves in a low oven, a necessity in busy households where most people worked outdoors. Work in the afternoon depended partly on the season, with a lighter workload during the worst of the

winter weather. Tea, in the late afternoon or early evening, after the second milking, usually brought the day to a close as people started to relax. Everyday tea was a miscellany of soup, eggs, cold meat, pies or salads, usually with bread and cakes. Baking was an important activity in a country kitchen. Special teas, for birthdays and social occasions, such as club meetings or cricket matches, included numerous types of sandwiches and fancy cakes as well as plain farmhouse ones.

This basic rural schedule varied according to the season, family custom and region. In some areas, the routines of growing grain demanded sustained bursts of outdoor work over several days, but not consistently early starts, except at harvest time, whereas raising sheep necessitated working long hours during seasonal lambing and shearing. The emphasis in country cooking on meat, cream, butter and animal fats in many recipes might seem unhealthy to us nowadays, but these were the basics to hand, and the calorie-dense dishes reflected the appetites of

many people who spent the best part of the day working outdoors. However, as you will see from many of the recipes in this book, the food was not always heavy. There were lighter dishes for summer, for special occasions and for variety, and some of these are also included. Most of the time food would be plainer and simpler, which is as true for, say, rural France as it is for the Yorkshire Dales, but this tends to be overlooked nowadays in our modern culture of easy abundance.

Basic food traditions are national but have regional nuances. Country traditions contain numerous variations on the theme of meat and potatoes, on small bread rolls and scones, and cakes large and small. Southwest England has a history of using pastry and clotted cream; the southeast has puddings in suet crusts; Wales has soupy stews and shares a tradition of cooking on a girdle (iron plate) with the Scottish Borders. Many Lake District recipes feature brown sugar and spices derived from the West India trade, which was once important to local harbours, while Yorkshire food includes oatcakes and oatmeal parkin. Fruit growing was regional, with the emphasis on apples and cider in the southwest and East Anglia; orchard fruit in Kent; and apples, pears and plums in the West Midlands. The north relied more on gooseberries and rhubarb, with damsons in the Lake District. Most kitchen gardens included pot herbs – leeks, cabbage and onions – but specialist foods, such as asparagus and watercress, were also grown in limited areas. Differences between regions come from their cooking methods, the availability of ingredients and local tastes, and this beautifully illustrated book reflects these in all their wonderful diversity.

Note
Most of the recipes require little in the way of specialist equipment; where this is needed it is specified. Several of the recipes in the baking section utilise a girdle (northern England and Scotland) – a heavy, perfectly flat iron plate or griddle, which is heated directly over a fire. Some hobs come with hotplates that can be utilised instead – or you can just use a heavy cast-iron frying pan.

Starters and
Light Meals

Bubble and Squeak Soup

SERVES 4 **This is good for showing off the potatoes and cabbage that southern Cornwall grows in vast amounts. The basic Cornish recipe closely resembles Portuguese *caldo verde*. For a vegetarian version, omit the bacon and use a little extra butter.**

Ingredients

30g (1oz) butter

115g (4oz) bacon, cut in strips

½ medium onion, finely chopped

900g (2lb) maincrop potatoes, peeled and cut in chunks

1 litre (1¾ pints) water

200g (7oz) spring cabbage

salt and pepper

100ml (3½fl oz) single cream

1 Melt the butter in a large saucepan and add the bacon. Cook gently until crisp, then remove and set aside. Add the onion to the fat and cook gently until soft but not brown. Add the potatoes and water. Bring to a simmer and simmer until the potatoes are soft; use a potato masher to break them down.

2 Discard the biggest outside leaves of the cabbage, plus any torn or discoloured bits and the chunkiest parts of the stems. Wash thoroughly and cut the largest leaves in half lengthways. Roll several leaves together in a tight roll and slice finely.

3 Add the shredded cabbage to the soup. Season to taste with salt and pepper. Cook gently for another 7–10 minutes, until the cabbage is tender. Add the cream and serve immediately with a scattering of the bacon pieces in each bowl. Some crusty bread goes well with this soup.

For a vegetarian version, omit the bacon

Green Pea Soup

SERVES 4 **This old family recipe originates from Wessex – Somerset to be precise – and although it was recorded by Florence White in the 1930s, it actually dates from the eighteenth century.**

Ingredients

850ml (1½ pints) water

285g (10oz) green peas (frozen are fine), plus an extra 100g (3½oz)

2 sprigs fresh mint or fennel, leaves only, plus extra to serve

1 celery stick, chopped

½ Cos lettuce, shredded

1 teaspoon salt

1 teaspoon granulated sugar

40g (1½oz) butter

½ cucumber, peeled, cut into quarters, deseeded and diced

½ large onion, finely sliced

1 tablespoon plain flour

1 Bring the water to the boil in a large saucepan and add 285g (10oz) of the peas with the mint or fennel, celery and Cos lettuce, plus the salt and sugar. Cook briskly for 20 minutes.

2 Purée in a blender or food processor or pass the whole lot through a mouli-légumes. Return the mixture to the pan, add the remaining peas and bring back to the boil.

3 In a separate pan, melt 30g (1oz) of the butter and add the cucumber and onion. Cook gently, without allowing them to brown. After 10 minutes, add to the soup.

4 Knead the remaining butter with the flour and drop it in small pieces into the hot soup, stirring well. It should thicken a little, but don't allow it to boil. Check the seasoning. Serve the hot soup with a little chopped mint scattered over the top.

A delicious bright green soup for spring

Spinach Soup

SERVES 6-8 **This light, elegant green and white soup is served with crisp golden croûtons.**

1 Sweat the turnips, onions and celery in the butter for 15 minutes. Add the chicken stock and simmer until soft. Put the mixture through a mouli-légumes or process to a purée. Return to the pan and add 700ml (1¼ pints) water. Return to a simmer and add the spinach, stirring slowly. Stir in the cream, seasoning and nutmeg.

2 To make the croûtons, cut the bread into 1cm (½in) cubes and fry in a little olive oil until crisp and golden. Drain well.

3 Pour the soup into bowls and serve hot, garnished with a few croûtons on each serving.

Ingredients

200g (7oz) white turnips, diced

200g (7oz) onions, finely chopped

200g (7oz) celery, finely chopped

knob of butter

565ml (1 pint) hot chicken stock

200g (7oz) spinach, shredded

55ml (2fl oz) single cream

salt, pepper and grated nutmeg

2 slices crustless white bread

olive oil

Stilton and Celery Soup

SERVES 4-6 **Stilton and celery often appeared together on the Edwardian cheese board, and this delicious combination has become a modern classic soup.**

1 Melt the butter in a large pan. Add the onion and celery and sweat gently for 30 minutes without browning. Stir in the flour, then add the stock and milk and simmer for 30 minutes.

2 Liquidise to a reasonably smooth texture (the celery will not break down entirely). Return to the pan and add the Stilton. Cook gently for a few minutes, stirring, until the cheese has melted. Taste and correct the seasoning. Serve with a little chopped parsley scattered over the soup.

Ingredients

55g (2oz) butter

½ onion, finely chopped

1 head celery, trimmed of any leaves and chopped

30g (1oz) plain flour

400ml (14fl oz) vegetable stock

400ml (14fl oz) milk

250g (9oz) blue Stilton, crumbled

salt and pepper

chopped fresh parsley, to serve

Ingredients

First stage

2 onions

2–3 large carrots

2 parsnips

1 medium swede or turnip

2 celery sticks

beef dripping, bacon fat or oil

500–750g (1lb 2oz–1lb 10oz) beef brisket

500–750g (1lb 2oz–1lb 10oz) boiling bacon, or a ham hock

a bouquet garni

pepper

Second stage

500g (1lb 2oz) small new potatoes, scraped

salt and pepper

½ small white cabbage, finely chopped

2–3 leeks, thinly sliced

chopped fresh parsley

Cawl

SERVES 8 **Cawl is a stew-like soup made with vegetables and cheap cuts of meat, such as boiling bacon, ham hock or beef brisket. It was the all-purpose everyday dish of Welsh farming communities, and everybody had their own version. It's impossible to make quickly or in small quantities, but if you want to feed a lot of people on a cold day it is ideal. Like most dishes of this type, it improves with reheating.**

1 Prepare all the root vegetables for the first stage by peeling and cutting them into rough cubes, about 2cm (¾in) square. Chop the celery roughly.

2 Melt the fat and brown the beef and bacon or ham, and transfer it to a very large pan in which you intend to cook the cawl. Next brown the root vegetables and add them to the meat. Add the celery and enough cold water to cover. Bring to the boil, skim, and add the bouquet garni and some pepper (no salt at this stage). Simmer gently for about 4 hours. At this point, the soup can be cooled and stored overnight if you wish.

3 For the second stage, remove the meat and carve it into neat slices, trimming off any fat and gristle. Return to the soup along with the potatoes and simmer for a further 20 minutes. Season to taste with salt and pepper.

4 About 10 minutes before serving, add the cabbage and leeks. Serve the soup in deep bowls, making sure that each serving has a few slices of meat. Sprinkle with chopped parsley.

Like most dishes of this type, it improves with reheating

Hotch Potch

Ingredients

500g (1lb 2oz) scrag end of lamb

1.5 litres (2½ pints) water

salt

3 small white turnips, diced

3 young carrots, diced

6 spring onions, sliced

250g (9oz) peas, fresh or frozen

4 best end of neck lamb cutlets

200–250g (7–9oz) broad beans
(shelled weight)

½ small cauliflower, separated
into small florets

1 small lettuce, sliced

chopped fresh parsley and mint,
to serve

SERVES 4 **This slowly cooked soup-stew is a traditional Scottish recipe, which can be traced back to the late eighteenth century and could be viewed as a summer version of barley broth. It is the sort of dish that can be left simmering very gently all day on a kitchen range – or, nowadays, an Aga. Otherwise, use the lowest possible heat on the hob, or cook in a slow oven. Cookery writers are united in saying that the slower and longer it is cooked, the better.**

1 Put the scrag end of lamb in a large pan and add the water and a teaspoon of salt. Bring to the boil, then skim, cover and cook on a very low heat for at least 1½ hours, preferably longer.

2 Drain the lamb stock off into a bowl and reserve. Lift out the scrag end, pick out any meat and discard the fat and bone. Clean the pan, and put the pieces of meat back in. Skim off and discard any fat that has risen to the surface of the stock, then return the liquid to the pan. Add the turnips, carrots, spring onions, half the peas and the lamb cutlets. Bring back to the boil and then simmer gently for at least another 1½ hours, until the vegetables are tender and the meat is well cooked.

3 To finish making the soup, add the remaining peas, the broad beans, cauliflower and lettuce and cook gently for about 30 minutes, until tender. Taste and add salt if required.

4 Serve in soup bowls, putting a cutlet in each, and scatter with chopped parsley and mint before serving.

Traditional Game and Lentil Soup

SERVES 4 **This is a substantial soup-stew to warm you up on a cold winter's day. You can serve it with crusty bread for a filling supper dish. It's a great way of using up the leftover meat from the carcass of a roast pheasant or partridge.**

1 Heat the olive oil in a large saucepan. Add the bacon, onion and garlic. Cook briskly for a few minutes, stirring all the time, until the onion begins to turn golden.

2 Add the celeriac, potatoes and herbs and cook a little longer, then stir in the lentils and pour in the stock. Bring to the boil, add any meat scraps and simmer gently for about 30 minutes, until the soup has thickened. Check that the lentils are soft – cook for a little longer if necessary – and season to taste with salt and pepper.

3 Serve the soup in 4 large bowls, scattered with chopped parsley and garlic and some fried breadcrumbs or croûtons.

Ingredients

2 tablespoons olive oil

115g (4oz) unsmoked bacon or pancetta, cut in 5mm (¼in) cubes

1 medium onion, chopped

1 garlic clove, crushed

½ small celeriac, cut in 5mm (¼in) cubes

2 medium potatoes, cut in 5mm (¼in) cubes

1 small sprig fresh rosemary

6 sprigs thyme

115g (4oz) green lentils

1–1.5 litres (1¾–2½ pints) game stock

leftover meat from roast birds, cut in small pieces

salt and pepper

To serve

chopped fresh parsley

1 small garlic clove, chopped

breadcrumbs or croûtons fried in unsalted butter

Serve it with crusty bread for a filling supper dish

Asparagus Tartlets

Ingredients

500g (1lb 2oz) asparagus

30g (1oz) butter, plus extra for greasing

salt and pepper

2 egg yolks

450g (1lb) shortcrust pastry (see page 298)

MAKES 18 Asparagus is grown all over Great Britain, but the Vale of Evesham in Worcestershire was always famous for their seasonal early-summer crop.

1 Wash and trim the asparagus stems, cutting off the hard ends of the stalks. Place the asparagus in a pan and just cover with boiling water. Simmer until the stems are tender. Drain well, cut off the tips and reserve them.

2 Put the rest of the asparagus in a processor or blender and blitz to a purée. Beat in the butter and season with salt and pepper. Stir in the egg yolks.

3 Roll out the pastry thinly and use to line 18 greased patty tins. Divide the asparagus mixture between them. Decorate with the reserved tips and dot with the extra butter.

4 Bake the tarlets in a preheated hot oven at 190°C, 375°F, Gas mark 5 for about 15 minutes. Serve warm.

Serve these delicious little tartlets warm

Leek Pasty

Ingredients

500g (1lb 2oz) leeks, trimmed, washed and sliced

plain flour, for dusting

butter, for greasing

450g (1lb) shortcrust pastry made with butter and lard (see page 298)

200g (7oz) lean ham or bacon, cut in small pieces

2 eggs

150ml (¼ pint) milk or single cream

pepper

beaten egg or milk, to glaze

SERVES 6

Leek puddings and pasties are a Northumbrian tradition. You can try substituting cheese for the bacon or ham for a vegetarian version.

1 Plunge the leeks into boiling water for a minute, then drain them in a sieve. Press a plate over the top to remove as much liquid as possible, and leave to drain while you prepare the pie.

2 On a lightly floured board, roll out two-thirds of the pastry thinly and use to line a greased Swiss roll tin. Scatter the ham or bacon over the bottom, and arrange the drained leeks on top.

3 Beat the eggs with the milk or cream. Add some pepper and pour over the leeks and ham. Roll out the rest of the pastry thinly and use to cover the pie. Seal, crimping the edges with a fork, and brush with beaten egg or milk.

4 Bake the pasty in a preheated hot oven at 200°C, 400°F, Gas mark 6 for 20 minutes, until the pastry is crisp and golden.

Substitute cheese for the bacon or ham in a vegetarian version

Cheddar Pork Pie

SERVES 4 **This Somerset recipe was collected in the area around the village of Cheddar by Mrs Arthur Webb. It is a pie in the sense that shepherd's or cottage pie is – the covering is potato, not pastry.**

1 Mix the flour with ½ teaspoon salt and some pepper and toss the pork in it. Smear the inside of a casserole with a little dripping and put in the pork. Add the stock or water and the apple brandy. Cover with a layer of apple rings, then onion, then potatoes; season these with a little salt and pepper and the sage. Then repeat, ending with a layer of potato.

2 Grease a piece of kitchen foil with some dripping and use to cover the pie tightly. Bake in a preheated moderately slow oven at 170°C, 325°F, Gas mark 3 for 2 hours.

3 Uncover the pie 30 minutes before the end of the cooking time, and turn the heat up to 190°C, 375°F, Gas mark 5 to crisp and brown the potatoes. Serve hot.

Ingredients

2 tablespoons plain flour

salt and pepper

500g (1lb 2oz) lean pork, cut in 1cm (½in) cubes

dripping or oil

150ml (¼ pint) stock or water

2 tablespoons apple brandy (if this isn't available, whisky is the best substitute)

2–3 sweet apples, peeled, cored and sliced in rings

1 very large or 2 medium onions, thinly sliced

4–5 large potatoes, peeled and thickly sliced

5–6 sage leaves, chopped

It is a pie in the sense that shepherd's or cottage pie is

Macaroni Cheese and Tomato Bake

Ingredients

225g (8oz) dried macaroni

salt and pepper

1 medium onion, chopped

1 tablespoon oil

400g (14oz) canned tomatoes, drained

4 teaspoons tomato purée

fresh basil leaves, roughly chopped

85g (3oz) butter

55g (2oz) plain flour

1 teaspoon mustard powder

425ml (¾ pint) milk

225g (8oz) Cheddar cheese, grated

SERVES 4 **Britain has always had a great affection for *maccheroni* (pasta tubes) – we even anglicised the name to macaroni, and at the beginning of the nineteenth century, dandies were called 'macaronis' because they wore wigs with white curls that were supposed to resemble macaroni. Macaroni Cheese has long been a supper standby. Combining the cheese sauce with fresh aromatic basil and tomatoes makes this dish especially appetising.**

1 Boil the macaroni in a pan of salted water, according to the instructions on the packet, and drain well.

2 Fry the onion gently in the oil and add the drained tomatoes, tomato purée and plenty of basil. Cook for a few minutes, breaking up the tomatoes with a wooden spoon and adding salt and pepper to taste.

3 Make the cheese sauce: melt the butter in a saucepan, then stir in the flour with the mustard powder and cook for a minute before pouring in the milk. Stirring all the time, bring to the boil and add 175g (6oz) of the grated cheese.

4 Stir the tomato and onion mixture into the cooked macaroni and spoon into 4 individual baking dishes or one large dish. Cover with the cheese sauce and then sprinkle the remaining grated cheese over the top.

5 Bake the macaroni cheese in a very hot preheated oven at 200°C, 400°F, Gas mark 6 for 20 minutes, or until golden.

Welsh Rarebit

Ingredients

200g (7oz) strong cheese, such as Cheddar or Cheshire, grated

30g (1oz) butter

1 teaspoon mustard powder

2 teaspoons plain flour

4 tablespoons beer

pepper

4 slices bread

SERVES 4

There are at least three basic versions of this classic toasted cheese dish. This is one of the more elaborate versions.

1 Put the cheese, butter, mustard powder, flour, beer and pepper in a small saucepan. Stir well and heat gently until everything is melted and well amalgamated.

2 Toast the bread on one side only and spread the hot cheese mixture over the untoasted side. Brown under a hot grill and serve the Welsh Rarebit immediately.

Little Cheese Puddings

Ingredients

6 thin slices white bread, crusts removed

butter, for spreading and greasing

115g (4oz) Cheddar cheese, grated

170ml (6fl oz) single cream

½ teaspoon mustard powder

pepper

a pinch of cayenne

freshly grated nutmeg

5 eggs, beaten

SERVES 6

These puddings are a bit like a baked Welsh rarebit. They were adapted from a much heftier Welsh recipe donated by Bobby Freeman.

1 Toast the bread on one side under the grill. Butter the untoasted side and line 6 individual ovenproof ramekins with a slice, toasted-side down, and cover with the grated cheese.

2 Bring the cream to the boil, add the seasonings and spices and beat in the eggs. Pour over the bread and cheese, and rest for 30 minutes.

3 Bake in a preheated moderately hot oven at 190°C, 375°F, Gas mark 5 for 20–25 minutes, until well risen and light brown. Serve immediately with a salad of watercress or rocket.

Duck Egg Frittata with Spinach and Butternut Squash

Ingredients

1 small butternut squash, peeled, deseeded and cut in 1cm (½in) cubes

40g (1½oz) butter

1 garlic clove, crushed

140g (5oz) spinach, picked over and washed

6 duck eggs or 8 hen eggs

pepper

½ teaspoon salt

55g (2oz) mature Cheddar cheese, coarsely grated

3–4 walnuts, chopped

SERVES 4

National Trust tenant Nikki Exton keeps ducks and devised this recipe to show off their eggs and the vegetables from her Dorset farm. The colours are fantastic, and it tastes good, too – duck eggs have a rich flavour. If you can't find them, use free-range organically produced hen eggs. It is important to cook duck eggs thoroughly.

1 Put the squash in an ovenproof dish with a little of the butter, then bake in a preheated very hot oven at 220°C, 425°F, Gas mark 7 for 20 minutes, until just tender.

2 Melt a little butter in a large frying pan and add the garlic, then the spinach. Stir gently until the leaves wilt dramatically and turn bright green. Remove from the heat when soft.

3 Beat the eggs, and add plenty of pepper, the salt and cheese. Stir in the cooked squash, spinach and garlic.

4 Over a high heat, melt the remaining butter in the frying pan. When it begins to foam, pour in the mixture. Stir it a little to begin the cooking process. Then turn the heat down very low and leave to cook gently for 10–15 minutes, by which time the frittata should be mostly set but slightly runny on top. Put a lid on the frying pan to complete the cooking: the frittata is ready when the top is set.

5 Scatter the chopped walnuts over the frittata. You can serve it hot, warm or cold, cut into wedges.

Baked Eggs with Tarragon

SERVES 4 **This recipe, devised with the produce of some of the National Trust's Dorset tenants in mind, makes an excellent starter or teatime dish, especially if you have good free-range eggs available.**

1 Take 4 individual ovenproof ramekin dishes and grease them lightly with a little butter.

2 Mix the cream and tarragon in a basin, and season lightly with salt and pepper. Divide between the buttered ramekins and then break an egg into each dish.

3 Bake in a preheated moderate oven at 180°C, 350°F, Gas mark 4 for 15–20 minutes, until the whites are set but the yolks remain soft.

Ingredients

butter, for greasing

120ml (4fl oz) single cream

2 teaspoons chopped fresh tarragon

salt and pepper

4 eggs

This makes an excellent starter or teatime dish

Glamorgan Sausages

Ingredients

250g (9oz) fresh white breadcrumbs

125g (4½oz) Caerphilly or Lancashire cheese, coarsely grated

55g (2oz) very finely chopped leek

1 tablespoon chopped parsley

6 sprigs fresh thyme (leaves only) or ½ teaspoon dried thyme

1 scant teaspoon salt

¼ teaspoon pepper

1 teaspoon mustard powder

2 eggs, separated

milk or water, to mix

plain flour, for coating

vegetable oil, for frying

MAKES 12

Traditional to South Wales, these are a mixture of cheese and breadcrumbs, seasoned with chopped leeks (or sometimes onions or chives). They make a good vegetarian alternative (cooked with vegetable oil, of course) to conventional sausages. The proportions, especially of cheese to breadcrumbs, vary from recipe to recipe – you can increase or decrease them according to taste.

1 Set aside 75g (3oz) breadcrumbs on a plate or in a shallow bowl. Mix the remainder with the cheese, leek, herbs, salt, pepper, mustard, both egg yolks and one of the whites. Stir well, and if the mixture seems dry, add a little milk or water – it should hold together but not be sloppy.

2 Flour a work surface generously, turn the mixture on to it and divide into 12 equal pieces. Roll each piece gently in the flour to make a sausage shape. Put the remaining egg white in a shallow bowl and whisk to break it up a little, but not until frothy. Put the plate or bowl of reserved breadcrumbs next to it. Pass each sausage through the bowl of egg white, then roll in the breadcrumbs until well coated.

3 Heat 2 tablespoons of oil in a large frying pan. Add half the sausages and cook gently, turning so that they brown and crisp all over. When they are golden, remove from the pan and drain on kitchen paper. Keep warm while frying the remaining sausages. These were traditionally eaten with potatoes, but a crisp green salad would make a lighter, healthier alternative.

Ingredients

225g (8oz) chicken livers

60g (2¼oz) butter

2–3 tablespoons Madeira

½ garlic clove, crushed

4 sprigs thyme, leaves only

salt and pepper

hot toast, to serve

Chicken Liver Paste

SERVES 4 **Chicken livers enjoyed a vogue as an ingredient in Edwardian cookery. Served whole or as pastes, they were used in rich 'savouries', little mouthfuls served on croûtons of fried bread that were thought to cleanse the palate at the end of a rich meal. This recipe is adapted from one given in *Cookery for Every Household*, written by Florence Jack in the early twentieth century. It is nicest eaten whilst still warm but remains very good chilled.**

1 Carefully check that the gall bladders (small dark green sacs) have been removed from the chicken livers and cut off and discard them if necessary. Also cut out any greenish stained patches. Divide each liver into 4–5 pieces.

2 Melt the butter in a small frying pan and cook the chicken livers very gently for 4–5 minutes, or until they are just cooked through. Towards the end of the cooking time, add the Madeira, garlic and thyme leaves.

3 As soon as the livers are done, tip the mixture into a blender or food processor and blitz until very smooth. Season to taste with salt and pepper. Divide the mixture between 4 ramekin dishes and serve, accompanied by slices of hot toast.

This is nicest eaten whilst still warm

Cornish Bacon and Spinach Pie

SERVES 4 **This pie is a recipe from the southwest and, like pasties, is another example of the Cornish habit of enclosing everything in pastry. This was originally done to make the food easier for working people to hold and eat in the fields or mines.**

1 Trim the bacon rashers of any excess fat and use a little of this to soften the chopped shallots in a frying pan. Blanch the spinach by plunging it into boiling water and draining well – put it in a sieve with a plate on top and press down hard to remove any excess water.

2 Use a third of the bacon to line the bottom of a pie dish. Cover with half the chopped spinach, scatter half the watercress and parsley over the top, then add the shallots. Cover with another third of the bacon, then add the remaining greenery.

3 Beat the eggs with the cream and a little pepper but no salt (the bacon will probably provide enough), and pour over the greenery. Top with the rest of the bacon.

4 On a lightly floured surface, roll out the pastry and use to cover the dish, crimping the edges to seal it. Bake in a preheated moderately slow oven at 170°C, 325°F, Gas mark 3 for 1 hour. Serve the pie hot.

Ingredients

250g (9oz) rashers bacon

3–4 shallots, finely chopped

250g (9oz) spinach, picked over and washed

1 bunch of watercress, chopped

1 handful of parsley, chopped

2 eggs, beaten

55ml (2fl oz) single cream

pepper

flour, for dusting

450g (1lb) shortcrust pastry made with butter and lard mixed (see page 298)

Potted Ham

SERVES 4 **This is a good way of using up leftover cold ham. Potting started off with raw meat cooked specifically for the purpose (it was actually a means of preserving, on a similar principle to French *confit d'oie*). Over the years, the recipes changed and became lighter and softer (and eventually evolved into the various 'pastes' sold as sandwich fillings).**

Ingredients

250g (9oz) cold cooked ham

pepper

ground mace, allspice or star anise

125g (4½oz) unsalted butter, softened

hot toast or crusty bread, to serve

1 Take a piece of cold ham and remove the gristly bits, skin and connective tissue, and any outside edges that have hardened and browned in cooking (these can all go in the stockpot). Fat (unless there is an excessive amount, which is unlikely these days) can be incorporated into the potting process.

2 Cut the ham into small chunks and then blitz it in a food processor. Add some black pepper and your other chosen seasonings. Mace and allspice are traditional; star anise isn't, but a suspicion, finely pounded, is good. Don't overdo the seasoning, and if you choose to add star anise, don't mix it with any other spices but black pepper, and add only a very small pinch – otherwise, it will be overpowering.

3 Beat the softened butter until creamy and mix in the seasoned ham. Put the mixture into a serving dish, such as a china soufflé dish, then chill in the refrigerator. Serve for lunch or tea, with hot toast or good bread.

A good way of using up leftover cold ham

Potted Shrimps

Ingredients

225g (8oz) butter

340g (12oz) brown shrimps, peeled

¼ teaspoon or 1 stick mace

¼ teaspoon freshly grated nutmeg

¼ teaspoon cayenne pepper

1 lemon, cut in 6 wedges, to garnish

hot toast, to serve

SERVES 6

Shrimps have a delicate flavour and are best eaten as soon as possible after they are caught. Potting enables us to enjoy them for a day or two longer. If you can't find brown shrimps, you can use this method to pot crab, prawns or flaked cooked salmon. The flavour of the seafood is very important; the fish needs to be fresh, not frozen then thawed.

1 First clarify 115g (4oz) of the butter. Cut it into small pieces and melt it gently over a low heat. Skim off any scum from the surface and pour off the clarified butter into a bowl. Leave behind the milky solids at the bottom of the pan. The clarified butter is now ready to use.

2 Melt the remaining butter in a pan that is large enough to hold the shrimps. Add the peeled shrimps, spices and cayenne pepper and heat through, stirring gently all the time. Do not let the mixture boil. Remove the mace and divide the mixture between 6 small ramekins. Spoon some clarified butter over each one, and then chill in the refrigerator.

3 To serve the potted shrimps, carefully unmould each pot on to a serving plate. Garnish with a wedge of lemon and eat with hot thin slices or fingers of wholemeal toast.

Use this method to pot crab, prawns or flaked cooked salmon

Main Courses

Slow-roasted Belly Pork with Apples and Onions

Ingredients

2–3 tablespoons oil

6 small onions or banana shallots, peeled

1kg (2lb 3oz) potatoes, cut in large chunks

500ml (18fl oz) light chicken or pork stock

salt and pepper

1 piece belly pork, about 1.5kg (3½lb), skin scored

few fresh sage leaves, torn up

6 small apples, preferably an aromatic variety, such as russets, peeled, halved and cored

SERVES 4-6 **This recipe was mentioned in the book *The English Housekeeper*, published around 1840.**

1 Put a generous tablespoon of oil in a large roasting tin, add the onions or shallots and potatoes and turn until they are well coated in oil. Pour in a quarter of the stock, then season with salt and black pepper.

2 Prepare the pork by drying the skin, then rubbing it with some of the remaining oil followed by a generous sprinkling of salt. Put a rack over the vegetables in the roasting tin and place the pork on it. Roast in a preheated hot oven at 220°C, 425°F, Gas mark 7 for 20 minutes, then reduce the heat to 150°C, 300°F, Gas mark 2 and cook for another hour.

3 Remove from the oven, lift the rack and add the sage leaves to the vegetables, stirring to ensure that they are well coated. Nestle the apple halves among the vegetables. Put the rack of pork back over the roasting tin and return to the oven to cook for a further hour. Again, remove from the oven and turn the heat up to 200°C, 400°F, Gas mark 6. Carefully lift off the rack of pork and stir the vegetables around once more. Replace the rack and return to the oven for a further 20 minutes.

4 Remove the pork and vegetables to a heated serving dish and use the remaining stock to deglaze the roasting tin, to make a thin gravy. Serve immediately with green vegetables.

Belly Pork with Root Vegetables and Oriental Flavourings

Ingredients

1 piece belly pork, about 1.5kg (3½lb), skin scored

salt

2–3 large baking potatoes, cut in chunks

1 large carrot, cut in chunks

1 sweet potato, cut in chunks

2 large parsnips, cut in chunks

2–3 small turnips, cut in chunks

1 tablespoon oil or pork dripping

6–8 garlic cloves, peeled

2.5cm (1in) piece fresh root ginger, peeled and cut in matchsticks

few shallots, halved lengthways

Oriental flavourings

2–3 whole star anise

1 teaspoon black peppercorns, lightly crushed

40g (1½oz) honey

2 tablespoons soy sauce

2 tablespoons dry sherry

200–300ml (7fl oz–½ pint) well-flavoured chicken stock

SERVES 4

Belly pork is a very economical cut of meat, and if you cook it really slowly it becomes tender and succulent with deliciously crisp crackling.

1 Preheat the oven to 220°C, 425°F, Gas mark 7. Dry the pork thoroughly and then salt it lightly. Mix all the oriental flavourings (only half of the chicken stock) in a small bowl.

2 Put the root vegetables in a pan, cover with cold water and bring to the boil for 2 minutes. Drain thoroughly. Heat the oil or dripping in a roasting tin until very hot, add the vegetables and turn them until well coated. Mix in the garlic, ginger and shallots. Pour the oriental flavourings over the vegetables, and put the pork on top, skin-side up.

3 Roast for 15 minutes, then turn the heat down to 150°C, 300°F, Gas mark 2. The meat can be left for 2–3 hours, although you may wish to stir the vegetables once or twice.

4 About 30 minutes before you want to eat, turn the heat back up to 200°C, 400°F, Gas mark 6. Stir the vegetables, being careful not to break them, then return to the oven. Check every 10 minutes or so to make sure the crackling doesn't burn. When it is crisp, remove the meat to a warmed serving platter. Arrange the vegetables around it. Keep hot.

5 Skim as much fat as possible off the juices left in the roasting tin. Taste and add more salt if needed, then pour the juices into a gravy boat. Use some of the remaining chicken stock to thin them and to deglaze any cooking residue in the roasting tin, then add to the juices.

Escalopes of Pork with Apples and Cider

Ingredients

4 thin pork escalopes

3 tablespoons seasoned plain flour

30g (1oz) butter

2 tablespoons brandy

100ml (3½fl oz) dry cider

2 apples, peeled, cored and thinly sliced

4 tablespoons double cream

salt and pepper

SERVES 4 **This recipe for local produce from south-west England was inspired by the French Normandy tradition of adding cream and apples to pork.**

1 Dip the escalopes in the seasoned flour. Melt the butter in a large frying pan and when it foams, add the pork and cook briskly, a couple of minutes per side. Remove to a warm plate.

2 Pour the brandy into the pan, scrape up any sediment, then ignite it and burn off the alcohol. Add the cider and the apple slices. Allow to boil and reduce the cider to a quarter of the original volume (remove the apple slices before this point if they become tender). Add the cream to the pan and stir thoroughly, allowing it to boil. Check the seasoning.

3 Return the pork and any accumulated juices to the sauce, then simmer for a minute or two and serve.

Cream and apples make a great accompaniment to pork

Roast Pork with Ginger and Madeira

SERVES
6 **This is not a traditional recipe, although the use of Madeira is a nod back to the late nineteenth century, when it was very popular in England.**

1 Leave the pork on a plate in the fridge overnight, uncovered; this is one way to encourage crisp crackling. Shortly before cooking, remove it from the fridge, rub the skin with a little olive oil and sprinkle with salt. Put the ginger and garlic in a roasting tin and place the pork on top (try to ensure it covers them or they will burn).

2 Put the pork in a preheated very hot oven at 220°C, 425°F, Gas mark 7 and roast at this temperature for 30 minutes, then add most of the Madeira to the tin and turn the heat down to 150°C, 300°F, Gas mark 2. Leave it to cook gently for another 2–2½ hours. Check occasionally to make sure it's not drying out (if it burns, it will taste bitter). Add the rest of the Madeira halfway through the cooking time.

3 When the meat is well cooked, lift it out of the tin to rest in a warm place. Drain the cooking juices into a heatproof bowl and pick out the garlic cloves. Spoon off as much fat as possible, then return a tablespoon to the roasting tin.

4 Mix over a low heat. Pour in the cooking juices and stir well, scraping in any sediment from the edges of the tin. Simmer until it thickens a little, then stir in the stock. Taste, correct the seasoning, and serve with some creamy mashed parsnip.

Ingredients

1 piece belly pork, about 1.5kg (3½lb), skin scored

olive oil

salt and pepper

20g (¾oz) fresh root ginger, peeled and cut in matchsticks

2–3 garlic cloves, bruised but not peeled

6 tablespoons Madeira

1 dessertspoon plain flour

250ml (9fl oz) hot chicken stock

Pork with Potatoes and Apples

SERVES 4 **This is really a pork version of a hotpot. Verjuice is the juice of unripe grapes and is available bottled from some delicatessens. It has a subtle sour-sweetness, good with all sorts of rich meat. If it is unavailable, a mixture of white wine and lemon juice in the proportions of about 3:1 is the best substitute. Use a potato peeler to peel off the lemon zest.**

Ingredients

4 spare rib pork chops, total weight about 800g (1lb 12oz)

1 medium onion

2 garlic cloves

8 juniper berries

a strip of lemon zest

salt

2 eating apples, suxh as Cox or russet

120ml (4fl oz) verjuice

800g–1kg (1lb 12oz–2lb 3oz) potatoes

about 20g (¾oz) butter

1 Put the spare rib pork chops in a deep ovenproof pie dish or casserole. Chop the onion, garlic, juniper berries and lemon zest together until quite fine. Mix with the pork, add a little salt, then cover and leave to marinate for 2 hours.

2 Peel and core the apples, then cut them into thin slices. Layer over the pork, and pour in the verjuice. Then peel the potatoes and slice them thinly as well. Use them to cover the pork and apples, sprinkling lightly with salt and dotting with butter as you go. Cover the top with a piece of buttered greaseproof paper or foil.

3 Cook in a preheated low oven at 140°C, 275°F, Gas mark 1 for 2 hours. At the end of this time, turn the heat up to 200°C, 400°F, Gas mark 6, remove the cover and allow the top layer of potatoes to brown and crisp.

Verjuice is the juice of unripe grapes

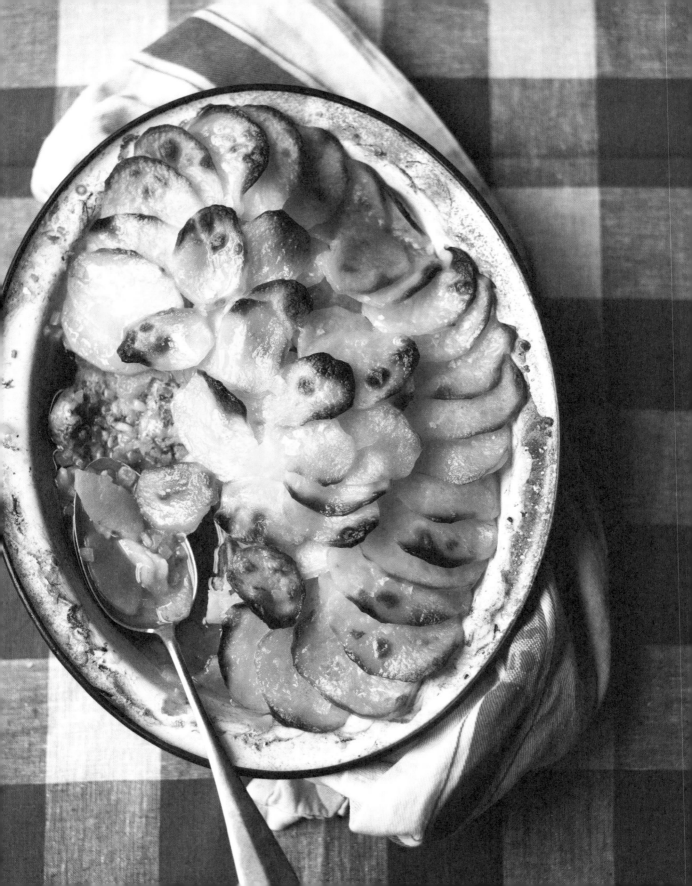

Ingredients

565–700g (1lb 4oz–1lb 9oz) lean pork fillet

a little butter

plain flour, for dusting

stock, wine or water, for the gravy

Sage and onion stuffing

55g (2oz) onion, finely chopped

30g (1oz) butter

115g (4oz) fresh white breadcrumbs

3 teaspoons chopped fresh sage

3 teaspoons chopped fresh parsley

salt and pepper

a little milk

Stuffed Pork Fillet

SERVES 4 **The idea for this delicious yet simple dish was sent from Northern Ireland to Florence White, when she was collecting recipes in the 1920s.**

1 To make the stuffing, cook the onion gently in the butter. Mix it with the breadcrumbs and chopped herbs, and season to taste with salt and pepper. Bind with a little milk.

2 Cut the pork fillet obliquely to give thin slices. If these don't seem to have a very large surface area, put them between sheets of baking parchment and beat them out a little with a rolling pin. Divide the stuffing between them, and roll each slice up, securing it with a cocktail stick or tying with kitchen string.

3 Butter a flameproof dish that will hold the pork rolls neatly and place them in it. Dust with flour and dot with a little more butter. Cook in a preheated hot oven at 200°C, 400°F, Gas mark 6 for 15–20 minutes.

4 Remove the cooked pork from the dish and keep warm. Add a little more butter to the cooking residues, and a dusting of flour. Deglaze the dish over a low heat with some stock, wine or water to make a little gravy. Serve with mashed potatoes and apple sauce.

An unusual take on a familiar meal

Slow-Roasted Shoulder of Pork

SERVES 16 **The essential ingredient for this is a very well brought up pig. At Heritage Prime in Dorset, Tamworths are reared for much longer than is usual, giving very large, well-flavoured joints. Scout round your local farmers' market for someone who raises a traditional breed to a high welfare standard, and buy a joint of pork with a decent covering of fat.**

1 Cooking time depends on size: a whole shoulder weighing 9kg (20lb) takes 24 hours, whereas a piece half that size will take 16 hours. However, the method works even on a relatively small joint if the cooking time is reduced proportionately. For example, give a piece of boned and rolled shoulder weighing 2kg (4½lb) 6–7 hours in the oven.

2 Take the pork out of the fridge an hour or two before cooking to come to room temperature. Preheat the oven to 240°C, 475°F, Gas mark 9. Make sure the skin of the pork is dry, then rub it with olive oil, salt and fresh thyme and place in a roasting tin; put a few sprigs of thyme underneath as well.

3 Put the pork in the hot oven and leave it for 20–30 minutes. reduce the heat to 140°C, 275°F, Gas mark 1 and leave it until almost the end of cooking time (a little longer won't matter). About 30 minutes before eating, turn the oven up to maximum again and then give the meat a final blast for 15–20 minutes. The crackling is wonderful and the meat has a melting texture. Serve with a salad of bitter leaves and some good bread.

Ingredients

1 shoulder of pork

olive oil

salt

sprigs fresh thyme

Pork Pie

Ingredients

1kg (2lb 3oz) pork, a quarter fatty, the rest lean

1 teaspoon salt

1 teaspoon anchovy essence

pepper

6–8 fresh sage leaves, chopped

Stock

2 pig's trotters

bones, skin or trimmings from the pie meat

1 bay leaf

2–3 sprigs fresh thyme

4 peppercorns

1 onion, stuck with cloves

3 litres (5 pints) water

Hot water crust pastry

450g (1lb) plain flour

½ teaspoon salt

150ml (¼ pint) water

55g (2oz) lard

55g (2oz) butter

30g (1oz) shredded suet

SERVES 10 **In the past, pork pies showed local variations in recipe and method and a good pie was a source of pride. Skilled pie-makers raised the crust entirely by hand, but a cake tin gives more certain results.**

1 Place the stock ingredients in a large pan and bring to the boil. Skim well and simmer, covered, for 3 hours. Strain the liquid into a clean pan and discard the debris. Boil the stock to reduce it to 500ml (18fl oz). Leave to cool and jellify, then chill.

2 Cut a quarter of the leanest pork into 1cm (½in) cubes. Mince the rest coarsely. Add the seasonings and sage leaves and turn well to evenly distribute them through the meat.

3 For the pastry, put the flour and salt in a large bowl. Heat the water and fats in a pan, stirring, until the water boils and the fat melts. Stir the mixture into the flour and, as it cools slightly, knead lightly. Cover the bowl and keep it in a warm place.

4 Take three-quarters of the pastry, still warm, and shape into a disc. Put it in an 18–19cm (7–7½in) round, sprung cake tin with a removable base and quickly raise it up the sides to the top. The dough should be malleable – if it flops, it is too warm. Pack in the filling. Roll out the remaining pastry to make a lid. Brush the edges with beaten egg. Trim any excess and crimp the edges. Make a small hole in the middle and cover it with a pastry rose. Cut pastry leaves to decorate the top. Brush with beaten egg.

5 Bake in a preheated hot oven at 200°C, 400°F, Gas mark 6 for 30 minutes. Lower the heat to 170°C, 325°F, Gas mark 3 and bake for 1½ hours. Don't worry if some gravy bubbles out. Remove the pie from the oven and let it stand for 20 minutes. Take the jellied stock, and if it has cooled off, reheat to boiling. Ease off the pastry rose and pour in as much hot stock as the pie will hold. Replace the rose and allow to cool. Wait 24 hours before cutting the pie into slices to serve.

Gammon Poached in Cider with Clove and Mustard Glaze

Ingredients

1.8kg (4lb) piece of gammon

450ml (16fl oz) cider

1 onion, 1 carrot and 1 celery stick for the stock

whole peppercorns

Clove and mustard glaze

2 tablespoons Dijon mustard

2 tablespoons soft brown sugar

a few whole cloves

SERVES
6

This combined method of starting by poaching and finishing with a blast in a hot oven seems to work perfectly with either large or small joints of gammon or bacon. Use the wonderful stock the ham produces to make a parsley sauce or some soup.

1 Place the gammon joint in a large saucepan. Pour in the cider and add sufficient water to cover. Add the onion, carrot and celery plus a few whole peppercorns. Cover the pan and bring the liquid slowly to the boil, then reduce the heat and simmer, very gently, for approximately 1 hour 40 minutes.

2 Strain off and reserve the stock. Turn the oven on to full heat. Line a roasting tin with baking paper and place the gammon joint in it. Slice off the skin, leaving a layer of fat on the joint. Smear the fat with the mustard and sugar and score with a sharp knife as if you were laying out a noughts-and-crosses game. Stud the pattern with cloves.

3 Pour in a little of the ham stock to stop the joint sticking and return it to the fully heated oven. Roast for 30 minutes, then turn off the oven and leave the joint to rest for at least 10 minutes. The ham is delicious sliced thickly and served with some parsley sauce.

Faggots

Ingredients

200g (7oz) onion, cut in chunks

200g (7oz) cooking apple, peeled and cored

200g (7oz) pig's liver, cut in chunks

200g (7oz) breadcrumbs

55g (2oz) shredded suet

20 fresh sage leaves, shredded

1 teaspoon salt and some pepper

1 pig's caul

butter, for greasing

a little well-flavoured stock

SERVES 4 **A prettier name for these meaty parcels is 'Savoury Ducks'. They are a way of dealing with some of the less glamorous bits of pig. Caul is a thin membrane with a lacy pattern of fat, which lines the stomach cavity of the animal; it wraps the mixture neatly, adds flavour and looks pretty. Not all butchers sell caul and you may have to ask around.**

1 Mince or process in a food processor the onion, apple and pig's liver. Mix in a bowl with the breadcrumbs, shredded suet, sage leaves, salt and pepper.

2 Soak the caul in a bowl of warm water. After a few minutes it should be soft and easy to spread out. Using some scissors, cut 12 neat squares from it, avoiding the fattiest bits.

3 Divide the liver and breadcrumb mixture into 12 pieces and wrap each one in a piece of the caul. Place them in a greased ovenproof dish and add a little stock.

4 Bake the faggots in a preheated moderate oven at 180°C, 350°F, Gas mark 4 for about 1 hour, until cooked right through and well browned.

These meaty parcels are sometimes called 'Savoury Ducks'

Pork Meatballs with Saffron Sauce

SERVES 4

This recipe was inspired by a dish of small pear-shaped meatballs, which appears in several cookery books of the late seventeenth and early eighteenth centuries. The original was based on veal, but the recipe works well with pork. The egg yolk and lemon juice thickening gives the sauce a pleasingly acid note, good with the rich meat.

1 Put the pork, breadcrumbs, thyme, parsley, lemon zest, cloves, 1 scant teaspoon salt and some pepper in a large bowl. Add the egg whites. Mix well and divide into 16 portions. For an authentically seventeenth-century look, roll into pear shapes, wider at one end than the other.

2 Heat a deep frying pan or a flameproof casserole. Add the saffron and let them toast gently for a moment – only enough to release their fragrance; don't let them burn. Pour in the stock and bring to the boil. Add the meatballs and simmer gently, turning two or three times, for 30–45 minutes.

3 Just before serving, beat the egg yolks with the lemon juice. Remove the meatballs to a warm serving dish. Off the heat, pour the egg and lemon mixture into the sauce. Heat very gently, stirring all the time, until the sauce has thickened a little and is thoroughly hot. Season to taste and pour around the meatballs. Garnish each with a sage leaf and stem, and serve with rice.

Ingredients

400g (14oz) minced pork

55g (2oz) fresh white breadcrumbs

leaves from 3–4 sprigs fresh thyme

1 generous tablespoon finely chopped parsley

zest of 1 lemon, and the juice of ½ lemon

¼ teaspoon ground cloves

salt and pepper

2 eggs, separated

a pinch of saffron threads

300ml (½ pint) pork or chicken stock

sage leaves and stems, to serve

Sausage and Green Lentil Stew

Ingredients

1 tablespoon lard, goose fat or olive oil

1 medium onion, finely chopped

leaves from 3–4 sprigs fresh rosemary, chopped

4 garlic cloves, chopped

600–700g (1lb 5oz–1lb 9oz) good-quality pork sausages

200ml (7fl oz) red wine

310g (11oz) small green lentils or Puy lentils

400ml (14fl oz) water

salt and pepper

1 tablespoon Dijon mustard

SERVES 4 **Our fresh sausages often lack the robustness and seasoning power of their European cousins, but are still good with lentils, echoing the long-time combination of pork with pulses. A well-made Cumberland sausage, meaty and highly peppered, is good for this recipe. If properly made, it should arrive coiled up in a long piece, rather than formed into links. Cut into suitable lengths before cooking.**

1 Heat the fat or oil in a heavy frying pan or flameproof casserole. Add the onion, rosemary and garlic and cook briskly, turning frequently, until the onion begins to brown in patches. Add the sausages and allow to cook gently, turning occasionally so that they brown a little all over.

2 Pour in the wine and let it bubble, then add the lentils, water and a little black pepper. Bring to the boil, then transfer to a casserole dish (if you used a frying pan) and cover with a lid.

3 Cook in a preheated moderately slow oven at 170°C, 325°F, Gas mark 3 for about 30 minutes. If the lentils seem to be drying out, add a little more water, preferably boiling. Return to the oven for another 20–30 minutes, after which the lentils should be soft but still holding their shape.

4 Mix the mustard through the casserole, then taste and check the seasoning – the sausages will probably have made the mixture salty enough, but add a little more as necessary. Serve with a salad of watercress and some good crusty bread.

Cumberland Sausage Coil in Beer

Ingredients

30g (1oz) beef dripping **or**
2 tablespoons oil

*500–600g (1lb 2oz–1lb 5oz)
Cumberland sausage in a long
coiled piece*

1 onion, sliced

1 tablespoon plain flour

*300ml (½ pint) beer, preferably
not too bitter*

salt and pepper

SERVES 4 **Cumberland sausages are a speciality of the Lake District. They should be full of coarse-cut meat and a bit of seasoning, and come in one long coil, not as links. They are excellent grilled or fried, but cooking them in beer produces a good gravy.**

1 Melt the dripping or oil in a large heavy frying pan or flameproof casserole in which the sausage will fit in a neat coil. Add the sausage and cook briefly on both sides, just enough to brown it. Remove it to a plate.

2 Add the onion to the fat and cook gently until softened but not brown. Sprinkle in the flour and stir well. Stir in the beer and let it bubble and reduce a little. Add the sausage and cook very gently for 30–40 minutes.

3 Taste the gravy and season with salt and pepper if necessary, but the sausage will probably have provided enough salt. Serve hot with mashed potatoes.

Serve this with creamy mashed potatoes

Irish Stew

Ingredients

310g (11oz) onion, coarsely chopped

1kg (2lb 3oz) neck of lamb (middle or scrag), cut into chops

310g (11oz) small white turnips, halved and sliced lengthways

1.2kg (2lb 11oz) potatoes, cut in large dice

salt and pepper

300ml (½ pint) stock (lamb for preference)

butter, for greasing

Garnish (optional)

a handful of fresh coriander leaves

1 small garlic clove, peeled

1 fresh hot green chilli, to taste

a little finely grated lemon zest

SERVES 4 **This is the ultimate comfort food – a simple, inexpensive dish known in the cookery of Ireland and Britain since at least the mid-nineteenth century. Irish Stew was originally made in a pan, cooked gently on top of the stove, and considered better if some of the potatoes began to dissolve into the mixture, thickening it. The best stews were said to be made with the minimum of water or stock. Cooking in the oven means it can be left to look after itself – but put it in a pan and simmer on the very lowest heat on the hob if preferred. It has a gentle, mild flavour; if you find it bland, try adding the garnish suggested at the end.**

1 Take a large casserole and build the vegetables and meat in layers, beginning with the onion and following with the meat, turnips and potatoes, then repeating until the ingredients are used up. Sprinkle 1 teaspoon salt and some pepper between the layers. Bring the stock to the boil, pour over the meat and vegetables and cover with buttered foil or paper and the lid.

2 Cook in a preheated moderate oven at 180°C, 350°F, Gas mark 4 for at least 2 hours, or longer on a lower temperature, if desired. A stew simmering on the hob will need checking occasionally to make sure it isn't drying out.

3 At the end of cooking, check the seasoning, and serve straight from the pot. To garnish, chop the coriander leaves, garlic and green chilli fairly finely, stir in the lemon zest and scatter a little of this mixture over each portion.

Hadrian's Wall Lamb with Root Vegetables

Ingredients

1 tablespoon oil
salt

700g (1lb 9oz) potatoes, cut in eighths

150g (5oz) turnips, cut in 1–2.5cm (½–1in) dice

150g (5oz) parsnips, cut in chunks

150g (5oz) carrots, thickly sliced

1 head garlic, cloves separated, peeled and left whole

1 small shoulder or 2 necks of lamb

4 sprigs fresh rosemary

8 sprigs fresh thyme

redcurrant jelly, to serve

SERVES 4 **Hadrian's Wall snakes across Northumberland, for some of its route following a ridge of hard rock known as Whin Sill. National Trust farms here produce grass-fed lamb and beef (both new season and wether (grown on to 18 months old) as Hadrian's Wall Lamb and Beef. Use a whole or half shoulder, or with neck of lamb, halved lengthways.**

1 Put the oil and ½ teaspoon salt in a roasting tin. Turn all the vegetables and garlic in the oil until well coated. Put the meat on top, tucking the rosemary and thyme underneath. Sprinkle with salt. Cover with foil, sealing it round the sides of the tin.

2 Cook in a preheated very hot oven at 230°C, 450°F, Gas mark 8 for 30 minutes, then turn the heat down to 140°C, 275°F, Gas mark 1 and leave it for 2½–3 hours.

3 Remove the lamb from the oven and turn the heat up to 220°C, 425°F, Gas mark 7. Put the meat on a warm plate and leave in a warm place. Discard the herbs. Pour as much of the fat and juice as possible out of the roasting tin into a bowl, stir the vegetables around gently and then return them, in the rosting tin, to the oven for 10 minutes to brown and crisp a little. Extract as much fat as possible from the juices.

4 Serve the meat, which will be falling off the bone, with the vegetables and pan juices, with some redcurrant jelly.

Herdwick Mutton with Salsa Verde

Ingredients

*1 leg of lamb or mutton,
about 2.5–3kg (5½–6½lb)*

salt and pepper

Salsa verde

*a generous handful each
of fresh mint, parsley, basil*

1 small garlic clove, crushed

2 tablespoons capers, rinsed

2 tablespoons Dijon mustard

2 tablespoons red wine vinegar

8 tablespoons olive oil

salt

SERVES 6 **Herdwick sheep have been grazing the Lake District fells for centuries and are now a rare breed. They have a distinctive appearance, with pale heads, small curved horns and rusty brown or grey fleeces. Their survival owes much to Beatrix Potter, a sheep farmer as well as a children's writer, who left her land to the National Trust on condition that Herdwicks were grazed on it in perpetuity.**

1 Put the lamb or mutton in a roasting tin and cook it very slowly in a preheated cool oven at 140°C, 275°F, Gas mark 1, allowing 1 hour per 500g (1lb 2oz). Season with salt and pepper towards the end of the cooking time.

2 Meanwhile, make the salsa verde: wash the herbs and pick the leaves off, discarding the stalks. Blend in a food processor or blender with all the other ingredients, or pound in a pestle and mortar. Season to taste with salt.

3 Carve the lamb in wedges, starting by cutting a slice halfway between the aitchbone (hip joint) and knuckle, then working outwards in each direction. Serve the salsa verde separately.

Carve the roast lamb in wedges

Shepherd's (or Cottage) Pie

SERVES 4 **This dish, the standard method for using up leftover roast lamb or mutton, seems to have first appeared in the 1870s, when mincing machines were developed. Cottage pie is the name that is usually given to the minced beef version. This is a basic recipe for either beef or lamb.**

1 Heat the fat in a large frying pan and add the onion and garlic. Cook gently without browning for 10–15 minutes. Chop the meat finely, or put it through a mincing machine (this will produce a softer texture).

2 Add the meat to the pan with the onion. Stir well and add the gravy, plus a little stock (or water) if the mixture seems dry. Check the seasoning, adding salt and pepper as necessary, then add some chopped parsley. Lightly grease an ovenproof dish and pour in the meat mixture.

3 Meanwhile, make the topping: peel the potatoes, chop roughly and boil until just tender. Drain and mash with the milk, butter, salt and pepper.

4 Cover the meat with the mashed potato, roughening the surface with a fork. Brown in a preheated moderately hot oven at 190°C, 375°F, Gas mark 5 for about 30 minutes.

Note: if you are cooking the beef version, Cottage Pie, try stirring 2–3 teaspoons of truffle oil into the mashed potato and sprinkle the top with grated strong Cheddar or Parmesan.

Ingredients

1 tablespoon fat from the roast, or oil

1 large onion, finely chopped

1 garlic clove, crushed

450–500g (1lb–1lb 2oz) cold roast meat (remove any skin, gristle, most of the fat and any bits of herbs left over from roasting)

300ml (½ pint) leftover gravy, plus a little stock

salt and pepper

1 tablespoon chopped parsley

butter, for greasing

Potato topping

1kg (2lb 3oz) floury potatoes

200ml (7fl oz) milk

30–40g (1–1½oz) butter

salt and pepper

Lamb Meatballs

Ingredients

400g (14oz) minced lamb

55g (2oz) fresh white breadcrumbs

1 garlic clove, crushed

1 tablespoon finely chopped fresh parsley

1 tablespoon finely chopped fresh basil

½ teaspoon grated nutmeg

salt and pepper

1 egg

30g (1oz) pistachio nuts, blanched (optional)

2 rashers fatty bacon (unsmoked), diced

10–12 small shallots, peeled

150ml (5fl oz) red wine

150ml (5fl oz) beef stock

2 teaspoons cornflour, blended with a little water

SERVES 4 **Recipes for meatballs appear in early English recipe books from the end of the sixteenth century until the middle of the eighteenth century. They were highly seasoned and enhanced with whatever spices, dried fruit and nuts happened to be fashionable at the time. This version is loosely based on recipes from the early eighteenth century.**

1 Put the minced lamb, breadcrumbs, garlic, herbs, nutmeg, 1 teaspoon salt, pepper to taste and the egg into a large bowl. Mix well, kneading everything together by hand.

2 Divide the mixture into 20 pieces, and form each one into a small ball (wet your hands in cold water to stop it sticking). If using pistachio nuts, seal one or two in the centre of each little ball. Heat a deep frying pan and add the bacon dice. Fry gently until they have yielded most of their fat. Add the shallots and meatballs and cook gently, turning occasionally, until the meatballs have browned on all sides.

3 Pour in the wine and let it bubble, then add the stock. Cover and cook gently for 30–45 minutes. Then stir in the cornflour mixture, heating gently and stirring all the time until the sauce thickens. Taste and correct the seasoning if necessary.

4 Serve the meatballs with some plain boiled rice or mashed potato and a dressed salad of bitter leaves.

Breast of Lamb with Capers and Herbs

Ingredients

2 breasts of lamb, boned

40g (1½oz) butter

1 medium onion, finely chopped

2 garlic cloves, crushed

2 tablespoons salted capers, well rinsed and coarsely chopped

a little chopped fresh mint

3 tablespoons chopped fresh parsley

1 tablespoon chopped fresh basil

finely grated zest of ½ lemon (preferably unwaxed)

150g (5oz) crustless day-old white bread, torn into small pieces

splash of stock or milk, to moisten

SERVES 3-4 **Breast of lamb needs slow cooking, moisture, and a highly flavoured stuffing to add interest and counteract the fattiness. In the past, standard English mixtures of bread with herbs and suet bound with eggs were favoured, but these are very dense to our modern tastes. We have borrowed flavours from salsa verde, which work well with this meat.**

1 Breast of lamb is flattish and thin, with one straight edge cut from the forequarter, which may still contain the ends of the rib bones, unless the butcher has already removed them. If you have to do this yourself, run a knife in between the bones and the meat on the outside, then cut them away from the lesser covering inside and slip them out.

2 Melt the butter over a low heat and fry the onion and garlic until softened. Stir in the capers, herbs, lemon zest and bread, and enough stock or milk to moisten the bread.

3 Spread the meat out, skin-side down. Put a layer of the lemony herb stuffing mixture on top of each piece, then roll it up from the narrow end and tie at each end with some string, firmly but not so tight that all the stuffing oozes out.

4 Put the lamb in a shallow roasting tin and cook in a preheated cool oven at 140°C, 275°F, Gas mark 1 for 3–3½ hours, pouring off any fat that the meat renders. Then turn the oven up to 200°C, 400°F, Gas mark 6 and cook fo a further 15 minutes to crisp up.

Braised Lamb Shanks

Ingredients

4 lamb shanks

*2 tablespoons olive oil,
plus extra for frying*

300ml (½ pint) red wine

salt and pepper

1 large onion, finely chopped

2 garlic cloves, finely chopped

*leaves from 1 sprig fresh
rosemary, finely chopped*

1 generous tablespoon plain flour

*a bouquet garni of a few sprigs
fresh parsley, marjoram, mint and
basil and 2 strips orange zest*

150ml (¼ pint) lamb or beef stock

SERVES 4 **Lamb shanks usually remained attached to roasts of lamb until the early 1980s, at which point a change in fashion liberated them to become foundations for dishes in their own right. Slowly cooked in rich, savoury sauces, they have now become a modern British country classic.**

1 Put the lamb shanks in a bowl and add the olive oil, red wine, 1 teaspoon salt and some pepper. Cover and leave the meat in the marinade for at least 2 hours (overnight is better). Turn the meat in the mixture occasionally. When ready to cook, drain the meat from the marinade, reserving the marinade for the sauce.

2 Heat a little olive oil in a flameproof casserole. Add the onion, garlic and rosemary and fry briskly, stirring frequently, until it is just beginning to turn golden. Pat the meat dry, toss it in the flour and add to the mixture, turning well until lightly browned. Dust in any remaining flour. Pour in the marinade, stir well and bring to the boil, stirring. Add the bouquet garni and the stock and return the mixture to the boil.

3 Cover the casserole with some foil and then with the lid. Cook in a preheated slow oven at 150°C, 300°F, Gas mark 2 for 2½–3 hours. At the end of cooking time, taste the sauce and add more seasoning if necessary. Serve immediately with creamy mashed potato or baked jacket potatoes.

Braised lamb shanks are a modern British classic

Lamb Steaks with Quince Jelly

Ingredients

a little olive oil

8 shallots, sliced

1 sprig fresh rosemary

30g (1oz) butter

4 lean lamb leg steaks, each weighing about 150–200g (5–7oz) or use neck fillet, cut in slices

4 garlic cloves, sliced

200ml (7fl oz) light chicken or beef stock

55ml (2fl oz) double cream

40g (1½oz) quince jelly

salt and pepper

a little lemon juice

SERVES 4

Mark and Charlotte Russell raise delicious lamb at Lanteglos, near Fowey in Cornwall. They sell some at their farm but to buy their lean steaks you'll have to go to Devon, to the Riverford Farm Shop, Staverton, near Totnes, where Ben Watson seams the leg meat into individual muscles. He suggested this great way of cooking them.

1 Put a little olive oil in a small saucepan. Add the shallots and rosemary and cook slowly until soft. Drain off any excess oil and discard the rosemary.

2 Melt half the butter in a large frying pan. When hot, add the lamb and fry rapidly on both sides until done to your taste. Remove and keep warm while you make the sauce.

3 Add the remaining butter and the cooked shallots to the pan. Fry quickly, then add the garlic and cook a little longer, but don't let it brown. Add the stock, turn up the heat and cook rapidly until syrupy. Stir in the cream and let it amalgamate. Then add the quince jelly and cook, stirring for a few moments to mix thoroughly. Check the seasoning and add a squeeze of lemon juice if desired. Serve with the steaks.

Quinces and lamb are natural partners

Traditional Liver, Bacon and Onions

SERVES 4 **Various recipes for hearty combinations of these three ingredients can be traced right back to the eighteenth century. This simple version makes an excellent and economical family supper.**

1 Mix the flour, paprika, pepper and salt together on a plate or in a shallow dish. Add the liver slices and turn them over in the seasoned flour until well coated. Set on one side.

2 Heat a large frying pan over a medium-high heat, add the bacon rashers and cook until done to your taste. Remove to a heated serving dish and keep warm. The bacon should have yielded enough fat to fry the rest of the ingredients, but if there is not enough, add a couple of tablespoons of oil.

3 Put the onion rings in the pan and cook briskly, stirring all the time, until they soften. Remove to the dish with the bacon and keep warm. Now fry the floured slices of liver in the same pan. Don't overcook them – 1–2 minutes on each side should be sufficient for really thin slices; slightly longer for thicker ones. Add to the still-warm dish of bacon and onions.

4 Quickly prepare some gravy, using the fat and residues left in the pan. First add the garlic and cook briefly without browning. Then stir in the flour left over from dusting the liver and cook for about 1 minute. Gradually stir in the beef stock to make a rich gravy (you may not need all the stock).

5 Divide the cooked liver, bacon and onions between 4 heated plates and serve immediately. Hand round the gravy and some mashed potato separately.

Ingredients

2 tablespoons plain flour

½ teaspoon paprika

1½ teaspoons pepper

½ teaspoon salt

300–340g (10½–12oz) lamb's liver, thinly sliced

8 rashers back bacon (preferably dry-cured), with quite a high proportion of fat

2 tablespoons oil (optional)

1 large onion, cut in rings

1 garlic clove, crushed

300ml (½ pint) hot beef stock

Lamb's Liver with Orange

Ingredients

30g (1oz) lard or beef dripping

1 large onion, thinly sliced

1 garlic clove, crushed

400g (14oz) lamb's liver, cut in thin slices

20g (¾oz) plain flour

fine slivers of orange zest and juice of 1 orange

about 150ml (5fl oz) strong beef stock

a pinch of chilli powder

salt and pepper

SERVES 4

Liver has gained a bad reputation in British cookery, probably as a result of school meals when it was served cooked to a texture like shoe leather. If stewed gently with plenty of seasonings until just cooked and tender, it is very different.

1 Melt the lard or dripping in a frying pan. Fry the onion and garlic gently until transparent, then remove with a slotted spoon and put on one side. Dust the liver with flour and fry lightly on both sides. Stir any remaining flour into the fat, then return the onion and garlic to the pan.

2 Stir in the orange zest and juice, the stock, a small pinch of chilli powder, 1 scant teaspoon salt and a generous grinding of black pepper. Stir well, then cover and cook on a low heat.

3 Test after 5 minutes by inserting the point of a sharp knife into one of the liver slices – if the juices run very red, cook for another 5–10 minutes but be careful not to over-cook it. Taste and add more seasoning if desired. Serve the liver with a bowl of fluffy mashed potato.

Take care not to over-cook the liver

Cornish Pasties

Ingredients

oil/butter, for greasing

plain flour, for dusting

225g (8oz) shortcrust pastry
(see page 298)

200g (7oz) potato, diced

100g (3½oz) raw turnip, chopped

70g (2½oz) onion, chopped

250–300g (9–10½oz) chuck steak
or skirt, finely chopped

salt and pepper

milk or beaten egg, to glaze

MAKES 2 **Pasties – also known as tiddy-oggies – are made all over Cornwall. Originally they were portable meals, taken to work by the tin miners and farm labourers, and had vegetables and meat at one end and a sweet filling for pudding at the other. We have used turnip here, but you can substitute thinly sliced swede. Don't used minced beef instead of steak.**

1 Preheat the oven to 200°C, 400°F, Gas mark 6. Lightly grease a baking tray or line with baking paper. On a lightly floured surface, roll out the pastry to 5mm (¼in) thick and then cut out 2 dinner-plate-sized rounds.

2 Mix the vegetables and use to cover half of each circle of pastry. Season the meat well and cover the vegetables. Wet the edges of the pastry and fold over the filling, crimping the edges to seal. Brush with milk or beaten egg to glaze.

3 Bake the pasties on the baking tray in the preheated oven for 15 minutes, then lower the heat to 180°C, 350°F, Gas mark 4 and cook for another 45 minutes, until golden brown.

Originally, pasties were portable meals

Beef, Guinness and Oyster Pie

Ingredients

55g (2oz) dripping or oil

1 large onion, chopped

2 garlic cloves, crushed

4 tablespoons plain flour

1 teaspoon salt and some pepper

750g (1lb 10oz) stewing beef, trimmed of all fat and gristle and cut into large cubes

400ml (14fl oz) beef stock

300ml (½ pint) Guinness

1 tablespoon chopped fresh thyme

1 tablespoon chopped fresh parsley

12 oysters

500g (1lb 2oz) puff pastry

plain flour, for dusting

1 egg, beaten, to glaze

SERVES 6 **The oysters are a subtle addition to this rich and hearty pie, but if you can't get any, don't worry – the pie will still taste delicious. Oysters can be quite tricky to open, so if you're nervous, why not ask your fishmonger to do it for you?**

1 Heat the dripping or oil in a flameproof casserole. Add the onion and garlic and fry gently until soft, about 20 minutes. Remove with a slotted spoon and put on one side. Mix the flour, salt and pepper and toss the beef in it. Brown it in the fat left over from frying the onion. Shake in any remaining flour and stir to absorb the fat. Return the onion to the pan and add the beef stock and the Guinness, stirring well, then add the herbs.

2 Cover the casserole and cook in a preheated low oven at 150°C, 300°F, Gas mark 2 for 2½–3 hours. When cooked, pour the mixture into a deep pie dish and allow to cool.

3 Just before cooking the pie, open the oysters and add the flesh and any juices (strained) to the beef mixture. Roll out the pastry on a lightly floured surface to 5mm (¼in) thickness and cover the pie. Scallop the edges with a sharp knife. Cut leaves for the top from the pastry trimmings, and glaze the pastry with beaten egg.

4 Bake the pie in a preheated hot oven at 220°C, 425°F, Gas mark 7 for 20 minutes, then reduce the heat to 180°C, 350°F, Gas mark 4 and bake for a further 30 minutes.

Steak and Kidney Pudding

Ingredients

40g (1½oz) dripping

1 large onion, chopped

3 tablespoons plain flour

salt and pepper

900g (2lb) lean stewing beef, cut in 2.5cm (1in) cubes

150–200g (5–7oz) ox kidney, trimmed and cut in 1cm (½in) cubes

400ml (14fl oz) beef stock

1 bay leaf

½ teaspoon ground allspice

splash of Worcestershire sauce

Suet pastry

340g (12oz) self-raising flour, plus extra for dusting

170g (6oz) shredded suet

salt

SERVES 4-6 **Mr Bristow, who farms near Redhill in Surrey on the southern slopes of the North Downs, produces superb quality lamb and Aberdeen Angus beef. Try the latter in this steak and kidney mixture, which is equally good in a pastry-topped pie.**

1 Melt a little of the dripping in a large pan and cook the onion gently for about 30 minutes, until soft. Remove to a casserole.

2 Mix 2 tablespoons flour, ½ teaspoon salt and some pepper, and toss the beef and kidney in it. Add the rest of the dripping to the pan and brown the meat. Add to the casserole.

3 Sprinkle another tablespoon of flour into the frying pan and gradually stir in the beef stock. Bring to the boil and cook for a few minutes, then pour over the meat. Add the bay leaf, allspice and Worcestershire sauce, then cover the cassrole. Cook in a preheated moderate oven at 170°C, 325°F, Gas mark 3 for 2 hours. Allow to cool.

4 Make the suet pastry: combine the flour, suet and salt to taste. Add enough water to make a coherent dough. Reserve a quarter of the dough for the lid and roll out the remainder on a lightly floured surface to a circle about 1cm (½in) thick. Use to line a 1.2 litre (2 pint) pudding basin. Add the filling, and roll out the remaining dough to make a lid. Cover the filling, pressing round the edges to seal. Cover with a double layer of greaseproof paper or foil, with a pleat to allow the pudding to expand during cooking. Tie securely round the rim of the basin with string.

5 Steam the pudding for 1½ hours, topping up the pan with boiling water if necessary. Pin a napkin round the basin and take it to the table to serve.

Pot-roast Brisket with Summer Vegetables

SERVES 4-6 **Brisket is now a very under-rated cut of beef, which is strange, because it not only has a lovely flavour but it also makes wonderful gravy, as showcased here in this delicious recipe.**

1 Melt a little fat in a flameproof casserole and brown the meat all over. Remove and put on one side, then add the spring onions and garlic to the fat and cook gently. When they have softened a little, pour in the red wine and let it boil for a minute or two. Add the carrots and thyme and sit the brisket on top. Sprinkle with the salt and pepper.

2 Cover the casserole dish with some kitchen foil and a tight-fitting lid. Cook in a preheated low oven at 170°C, 325°F, Gas mark 3 for about 2½ hours.

3 At this point, uncover the casserole. The meat will have produced lots of gravy. Add the peas and beans. Seal the pot again and continue cooking for another 30–40 minutes. Remove the meat to a warm dish. Skim the gravy if it seems to have a lot of fat on top. Combine the cornflour or arrowroot with a little cold water and add to the gravy, bring to the boil and stir while it thickens. Taste and correct the seasoning.

Ingredients

dripping, oil or bacon fat

lkg (2lb 3oz) brisket, boned and rolled

1 bunch spring onions, chopped

1 garlic clove, crushed

150ml (¼ pint) red wine

200g (7oz) young carrots, topped and tailed (if they are really young, they won't need peeling)

1 sprig freh thyme

1 teaspoon salt and some pepper

100g (3½oz) shelled fresh peas

150–200g (5–7oz) green beans, cut in short lengths

2 teaspoons cornflour or arrowroot

A Welsh Stew

Ingredients

*about 500g (1lb 2oz) stewing
beef, trimmed of any gristle and
fat, and cut into slices about
4cm (1½in) square*

400ml (14fl oz) beef stock

8 leeks

*310g (11oz) small white turnips
(or use a slice from a large one)*

salt and pepper

a pinch of sugar

chopped fresh parsley, to serve

SERVES 4

**Eliza Acton gave this lovely recipe in her book
Modern Cookery for Private Families (1845).
It is recognisably a version of cawl, a soup-like stew
of meat and vegetables traditional to Welsh cookery
(see page 18). Acton's version is simple but refined.
The better the beef and the stock, the better the dish.**

1 Put the beef and stock in a flameproof casserole and bring
to a simmer. Cover and cook in a preheated moderate oven
at 180°C, 350°F, Gas mark 4 for 1 hour.

2 Prepare the vegetables: cut the white part off the leeks, trim
and wash and cut into slices about 2cm (¾in) long (this will
probably leave quite a lot of green, the best of which can be
used for soup). Peel the turnips: small ones can be cut into
quarters; if using a piece of a large one, cut as if making chips.

3 After 1 hour, remove the casserole from the oven. The beef
should be fairly tender and the stock well flavoured. Add
the prepared vegetables, 1 teaspoon salt, pepper to taste and
a pinch of sugar. Return to the oven for about 1¼ hours. Stir
occasionally during this time.

4 Check the seasoning and divide the stew between 4 shallow
soup plates. Sprinkle each portion with parsley and serve
with floury potatoes, boiled or steamed.

A simple, delicious stew
of beef, leeks and turnips

Beef Stew with Dumplings

Ingredients

55g (2oz) beef dripping, lard or oil, plus a little extra

1 large onion, sliced

2 garlic cloves, crushed

150g (5oz) turnip, diced

1 large parsnip, cubed

1 large carrot, cubed

salt and pepper

40g (1½oz) flour

450–500g (1lb–1lb 2oz) lean stewing beef, cut into cubes

250ml (9fl oz) beef stock

250ml (9fl oz) mild beer (use beef stock or wine instead if desired)

1 bay leaf

a few sprigs fresh marjoram or 1 teaspoon dried marjoram

Dumplings

1 quantity dumpling mix (see page 301)

horseradish, or mustard and parsley, as flavourings

SERVES 4 **This stew has been a mainstay of English domestic cookery since the mid-nineteenth century. Make it with any cut of beef, cook it with stock or beer and then add root vegetables and dumplings. Comfort food for the coldest winter day.**

1 Heat the fat in a frying pan. Fry the onion and garlic until softened. Remove and add to a casserole. Fry the root vegetables for a few minutes, then add to the onion.

2 Mix 1 teaspoon salt with some pepper and the flour and toss the beef into it. Brown the meat in the remaining fat, then add to the vegetables in the casserole.

3 Sprinkle the remaining seasoned flour into the pan. Add the stock, stirring well and scraping any bits of sediment off the bottom. Stir in the beer and bring to the boil. Pour over the meat and vegetables, then add the bay leaf and marjoram. Cover and cook in a preheated oven at 150°C, 300°F, Gas mark 2 for 2 hours.

4 Make the dumplings as per the recipe on page 301, using horseradish or mustard and parsley as flavourings.

5 Remove the casserole from the oven and skim off any excess fat. Check the seasoning and arrange the dumplings on top. Turn the heat up to 180°C, 350°F, Gas mark 4 and return the dish, uncovered, to the oven for about 20 minutes, or until the dumplings are cooked and starting to crisp slightly on top.

Stewed Steak

SERVES 4 **There are many recipes for stewing or braising steak, many of which are similar in that they rely on combinations of store-cupboard ingredients – vinegar, and ready-made sauces, such as mushroom ketchup or Worcestershire sauce – to produce a strongly flavoured gravy. This updated version, which uses balsamic vinegar, shares the characteristics of similar recipes from the past, as it is quick and simple to put together and good to eat on a cold day.**

1 Put the braising steak in a shallow ovenproof dish along with the garlic and star anise. Mix together the soy sauce, balsamic vinegar and tomato juice, and pour over the steak. Cover the dish with foil and then with a lid if the dish has one.

2 Cook in a preheated low oven at 140°C, 275°F, Gas mark 1 for 3 hours, by which time the meat should be extremely tender and surrounded by a well-flavoured sauce. Serve with a mixture of potato and parsnip mashed together.

Ingredients

500g (1lb 2oz) braising steak, cut in slices about 2cm (¾in) thick

4 garlic cloves, peeled

1 whole star anise

4 tablespoons dark soy sauce

2 tablespoons balsamic vinegar

200ml (7fl oz) tomato juice

This casserole is good to eat on a cold day

Lobscouse with Parsley Dumplings

Ingredients

500g (1lb 2oz) good-quality braising steak

200g (7oz) young carrots, halved lengthways

200g (7oz) small white turnips, cut into batons

4 garlic cloves, peeled

a bouquet garni of 1 bay leaf, 1 sprig fresh rosemary and a few sprigs fresh thyme

300–400ml (10–14fl oz) water

salt and pepper

800g (1lb 12oz) new potatoes, scrubbed

Suet dumplings

1 quantity dumpling mix (see page 301)

1 teaspoon mustard powder

a pinch of cayenne pepper

1 tablespoon chopped fresh parsley

SERVES 4

Lobscouse is a type of stew made around the coasts of north-west Europe, including the port of Liverpool. That's why Liverpudlians are known as scousers. Beef, fresh or salted, is the usual principal ingredient, although fish versions are also known. Tender summer carrots, small white turnips and new potatoes are used in this summer version; winter root vegetables give a more robust flavour.

1 Trim the meat of any obvious fat and gristle, and cut it into 2.5cm (1in) cubes. Put the carrots, turnips and garlic in a layer over the bottom of a large saucepan. Tuck the bouquet garni in among them. Add the beef in a layer on top. Pour in enough water to cover the vegetables and add some salt and pepper.

2 Cover tightly with a layer of foil under the lid, and put the pan on the lowest heat. Simmer gently for 1 hour, making sure the liquid doesn't boil away. Then uncover the stew, add the potatoes (cut into halves or quarters if they are large), cover again and continue to cook for about 20 minutes.

3 Towards the end of cooking, make the dumplings (see page 301), mixing the mustard, cayenne and parsley into the flour. Uncover the stew, remove the herbs, taste the liquid and add more seasoning if necessary. Drop the dumplings on top of the mixture, re-cover and simmer for another 20 minutes.

Roast Beef and Yorkshire Pudding

SERVES 6 **A family favourite for Sundays and holidays. The secret of successful Yorkshire pudding is to get the fat sizzling hot before adding the batter, and not to open the oven door while it is cooking.**

Ingredients

1.5–2kg (3½–4½lb) sirloin or rib roast, or wing rib or forerib

salt and pepper

Yorkshire pudding

2 eggs, beaten

100g (3½oz) plain flour

a pinch of salt

250ml (9fl oz) milk and water mixed half and half

beef dripping from the roast

1 Allow the beef to come to room temperature before cooking, and season with salt and pepper. Place in a roasting tin and cook in a preheated hot oven at 240°C, 475°F, Gas mark 9 for 15 minutes, then reduce the heat to 180°C, 350°F, Gas mark 4 and allow 15 minutes per 500g (1lb 2oz) for rare beef or 18–20 minutes for medium-cooked (on the bone); or 12 minutes (rare) and 13–15 minutes (medium) for boneless. Rest the beef for 20–30 minutes while you make the Yorkshire pudding and gravy.

2 As soon as the beef goes into the oven, make the Yorkshire pudding batter: mix the eggs, flour and salt until smooth. Blend in the milk and water to give the batter the consistency of thin cream. Leave to stand for at least 1 hour.

3 When the beef is out of the oven, turn the heat up to 220°C, 425°F, Gas mark 7. Add a tablespoon of dripping to a 23cm (9in) pudding tin and heat it in the oven until smoking hot. Pour in all but 2 tablespoons of batter (it will hiss spectacularly if the fat is the right temperature) and put the pudding in the oven. Cook for about 20 minutes, until well risen and browned.

4 Meanwhile, make the gravy: spoon off any excess fat from the roasting tin. Scrape up the sediment using the meat juices and make up the amount of liquid to about 200ml (7fl oz) with vegetable water or stock. Let it bubble, then take off the heat and stir in the reserved Yorkshire pudding batter. Keep stirring until the mixture thickens. Add a little more liquid as appropriate, then season to taste. Serve with the carved roast beef and Yorkshire pudding.

Shin of Beef in Branscombe Bitter

Ingredients

3 tablespoons plain flour

salt and pepper

565g (1¼lb) shin of beef,
thickly sliced

2 rashers dry cure bacon,
cut in matchsticks

30g (1oz) butter or
2 tablespoons oil (optional)

1 garlic clove, crushed

250g (9oz) small onions, peeled

400ml (14fl oz) bitter beer

1 teaspoon brown sugar

½ teaspoon English mustard

SERVES 4

The National Trust owns the Branscombe Vale Brewery in Devon. We used their Drayman's Best Bitter, a smooth, hoppy beer, for this casserole.

1 Mix the flour with a scant teaspoon of salt and plenty of black pepper, and turn the beef over in it until lightly coated.

2 Heat a flameproof casserole and cook the bacon gently, adding butter or oil if it doesn't yield much fat. Remove the bacon and brown the floured beef in the fat. Add the garlic and cook briefly before adding the onions. Stir in any remaining flour and return the bacon to the pan. Add the beer and let it bubble. Stir in the sugar and mustard.

3 Cover the casserole and cook very gently in a preheated slow oven at 150°C, 300°F, Gas mark 2 for 3 hours, then remove and cool. The stew is much better left until the following day, when you can easily lift any solidified fat off the top. Reheat gently and serve with baked potatoes and glazed carrots.

Use any smooth bitter beer in this piquant casserole

Carlisle Steak

SERVES
4

This is an updated version of a dish from the Lake District, which Mrs Arthur Webb noted as 'guaranteed to keep out the chilliest cold' when she came across it in the 1930s. Well-matured rump steak is best for both flavour and texture, but the meat will need to be marinated for 6–12 hours.

1 Mix the vinegar, soy sauce, sugar, beer and allspice in a wide shallow bowl and put the steaks in it. Cover and put to one side; turn the meat from time to time. When you are ready to cook the meat, lift it out and allow the liquid to drain off for a few minutes. Reserve the marinade.

2 Blot the steaks dry with kitchen paper and dust with flour. Heat a smear of oil in a heavy frying pan, and, when hot, add the steaks. Allow to sizzle for a few minutes, and then turn them over and continue cooking until they are done to your taste. Remove from the pan and let them rest on a warm plate while you make the sauce.

3 Add the butter to the steak cooking residues. When it has melted, stir in the tablespoon of flour. Add the marinade, stirring well to incorporate everything. Add a little stock or water if it seems too thick. Pour over the steaks and garnish with chopped parsley. Serve with creamy mashed potato.

Ingredients

4 tablespoons malt vinegar

4 tablespoons dark soy sauce

1 tablespoon muscovado sugar

100ml (3½fl oz) bitter beer

½ teaspoon ground allspice

4 pieces lean rump steak

1 tablespoon plain flour, plus extra for dusting

oil, for frying

30g (1oz) butter

a little stock or water (optional)

chopped fresh parsley, to serve

Ragoût of Oxtail

Ingredients

salt and pepper

2 oxtails, cut in pieces

1 medium onion, finely chopped

2 garlic cloves, crushed

2 bay leaves, spines removed, the remainder finely shredded

1 tablespoon chopped fresh parsley

leaves of 3–4 sprigs thyme

565ml (1 pint) red wine

200g (7oz) unsmoked pancetta or good bacon, diced

250g (9oz) carrot, diced

250g (9oz) mushrooms, finely sliced

1 generous tablespoon truffle paste (optional)

500g (1lb 2oz) shallots, peeled

450ml (16fl oz) beef stock

40g (1½oz) plain flour

40g (1½oz) butter

SERVES 6

Oxtail is a delicious but sadly under-rated cut, which is now rarely used. It makes delicious stews and casseroles flavoured with stock or wine.

1 Dissolve 1 tablespoon salt in cold water, then soak the oxtail pieces in it for about 1 hour. Drain well. Put the oxtail in a deep bowl. Mix the onion, garlic, bay leaves, parsley, thyme, a generous quantity of pepper and the wine, and pour over the meat. Cover and leave to marinate for at least 4 hours.

2 When ready to cook the stew, take a large flameproof casserole and set it over a low heat. Add the pancetta or bacon and cook until starting to crisp. Put the carrot and mushrooms on top (no need to stir), and add the truffle paste, if using. Then add the pieces of meat in a layer, and tuck the shallots into the spaces in between.

3 Pour the marinade over, turn up the heat and let it bubble. Add the beef stock and 1 teaspoon salt. Bring to the boil, skim off any scum, then cover with foil and a lid. Cook in a preheated cool oven at 140°C, 275°F, Gas mark 1 for 4 hours.

4 At the end of the cooking time, remove from the oven and skim off as much fat as possible. Check the seasoning. Knead the flour and butter together and dot small pieces of this over the surface of the liquid (remove the pieces of oxtail to a hot serving dish if they seem to be in the way). Heat gently and stir until the sauce has thickened. Serve with mashed potato or a purée of potato and celeriac.

Braised Ox Cheek, Cloves and Oranges

Ingredients

600–700g (1lb 5oz–1lb 9oz) ox cheek, cut to give 3–4 thick slices from each one

225ml (8fl oz) red wine

150ml (¼ pint) well-flavoured beef stock

1 orange

6 cloves

freshly grated nutmeg

salt and pepper

20g (¾oz) flour

20g (¾oz) butter, softened

SERVES 4

Ox cheek is cheap and well flavoured but needs gentle cooking. This recipe also works well with braising steak or escalopes – shorten the cooking time accordingly. The key is to use strong beef stock (home-made if possible) or a good ready-made one, and reduce it to concentrate the flavour. Good gravy left over from a roast of beef could also be used.

1 Put the ox cheek in a shallow ovenproof dish. Mix the wine and stock. Remove 4–5 strips of zest from the orange with a canelle knife or a potato peeler and add them, along with the cloves and a generous grating of nutmeg. Grind in a little black pepper, add about ½ teaspoon salt, and bring the mixture to a simmer. Pour over the beef.

2 Cover the dish tightly with foil and a lid if it has one. Cook in a preheated low oven at 140°C, 275°F, Gas mark 1, or even lower if possible, for 3–3½ hours.

3 Remove the meat to a warm serving dish. Add the juice of half the orange, or more to taste, plus extra salt and pepper as desired, to the liquid in the casserole dish.

4 Knead the flour and butter together and dot over the surface of the sauce, so it melts into the liquid. The sauce may need to be briefly reheated, but don't overdo this – just enough to thicken it lightly. Serve the ox cheek with a very creamy purée of potato, or some plain steamed potatoes.

Veal Olives

SERVES 4 **These thinly rolled slices of veal were used as pie fillings in the seventeenth and eighteenth centuries, but they are very good on their own with a little sauce. The name has nothing to do with olives but is derived from a French word for lark: the meat rolls, plumply stuffed, are reminiscent of small birds.**

1 Lay the veal escalopes out on a large flat plate or board and then cover each one with a slice of Parma ham.

2 Put the breadcrumbs in a bowl. Melt the butter and crush the anchovies into it. Pour into the breadcrumbs, add the thyme, lemon, mace and some pepper. Mix in the egg and stir well, then divide into four and spread each portion over the ham on top of the escalopes. Roll up, enclosing the stuffing, and tie each olive with thread in 2 or 3 places.

3 Melt a little butter in a flameproof casserole and fry the olives briefly, just enough to brown them lightly all over. Remove to a plate. Add the sliced mushrooms to the pan and fry over a fairly high heat, stirring well, until they brown a little. Put the rolls of meat back in, pour in the sherry and let it bubble. Add the stock and bring to a simmer, then cover the pan.

4 Cook the olives in a preheated moderate oven at 150°C, 300°F, Gas mark 2 for 1 hour. Serve with plain boiled rice.

Ingredients

4 veal escalopes, each weighing about 100g (3½oz)

4 slices Parma ham

100g (3½oz) fresh breadcrumbs

55g (2oz) butter, plus a little extra for frying

2 anchovies

leaves of 3–4 sprigs fresh thyme

finely grated zest of ½ lemon

½ teaspoon ground mace

pepper

1 small egg, beaten

200g (7oz) button mushrooms, trimmed and sliced

120ml (4fl oz) dry sherry

120ml (4fl oz) veal or chicken stock

Spring Veal Stew with Gooseberries

Ingredients

450–500g (1lb–1lb 2oz) stewing veal, cut in 2cm (¾in) cubes

30g (1oz) plain flour

40g (1½oz) butter

6 spring onions, trimmed and cut in 2cm (¾in) lengths

140g (5oz) green gooseberries

345ml (12fl oz) hot veal or chicken stock

salt and pepper

½ cucumber, peeled, deseeded and cut in 1cm (½in) dice

2 Little Gem lettuces, outer leaves removed, trimmed and cut in quarters lengthways

chopped fresh chives, to garnish

SERVES 4

In summer, English cooks liked to pair veal with fresh greenery and slightly acid flavours. Sorrel was often chosen, but this unusual combination of cucumber, lettuce and gooseberries was suggested by Eliza Acton in 1845. She cooked everything together from the start, but the vegetables become very soft this way, so put them in about halfway through cooking to retain some of their texture.

1 Toss the veal in the flour. Melt the butter in a frying pan or flameproof casserole. Add the veal and fry briskly to brown. Add the spring onions and gooseberries and continue frying for a few minutes. Stir in any remaining flour, then add the stock, stirring well to make a sauce. Add ½ teaspoon salt and a little pepper. Cover the pan and simmer gently for about 1 hour, stirring occasionally.

2 Add the cucumber and lettuce. Cover and cook for a further 1 hour, or until the meat is tender and the vegetables are cooked. Stir, check the seasoning, and garnish with a scatter of chopped chives. Serve with new potatoes.

This unusual flavour combination is surprisingly good

Coronation Chicken

Ingredients

1 chicken, weighing about
1.5–1.8kg (3½–4lb), cooked
and cooled

1 tablespoon sunflower oil

1 small onion, finely chopped

1cm (½in) cube fresh root ginger,
peeled and grated

1 tablespoon curry powder
(old-fashioned Madras type)

2 heaped tablespoons mango
chutney (chop up any large
pieces of fruit)

150ml (¼ pint) mayonnaise

115g (4oz) plain yoghurt (use
full-fat or Greek-style, if a richer
result is desired)

salt and pepper

55g (2oz) flaked almonds

fresh parsley or coriander sprigs,
to garnish

SERVES 6 **The original recipe for this dish was devised by the Cordon Bleu Cookery School in London for the coronation of Queen Elizabeth II. For a truly special summer meal, it is worth roasting a top-quality chicken to make this. Adding yoghurt to the sauce reduces the fat content and makes it lighter.**

1 Skin, joint and bone the chicken into neat serving pieces and arrange on a platter. Keep cool while you prepare the sauce.

2 Heat the oil in a small frying pan. Add the onion and ginger and cook over a low heat for 5–10 minutes, until the onion is soft and translucent. Stir in the curry powder and continue cooking gently for 1–2 minutes. Scrape the mixture into a bowl and set aside to cool.

3 When the onion mixture is cool, stir in the mango chutney, mayonnaise and yoghurt, then add a little water to thin the sauce to a coating consistency. Taste and correct the seasoning, then spoon this sauce over the chicken.

4 Toast the almonds gently in a low oven until golden brown. Allow them to cool, then scatter over the top of the chicken and garnish with parsley or coriander. Keep in a cool place or the refrigerator until ready to serve.

It's worth roasting a top-quality chicken for this classic dish

Devilled Chicken

Ingredients

*1 chicken, weighing about
1.5–1.8kg (3½–4lb), jointed*

salt

300ml (½ pint) single cream

*1 tablespoon Madras curry
powder*

1 tablespoon mustard powder

SERVES 4-6

**Surrey and Sussex were famous for chickens
and capons up until World War II. In those days,
they were quite expensive and considered a treat.
'Devilling' poultry in a spicy sauce was popular in
the nineteenth and early twentieth centuries.**

1 Season the chicken joints with salt and cook them under
a hot grill, turning frequently, for 15–20 minutes, until the
juices run clear when the thickest part is pierced with a skewer.
The chicken can be baked but will not be as succulent.

2 Mix the cream, curry powder and mustard in a frying pan.
Add the pieces of chicken and any meaty juices from the
grill pan. Heat gently – the mixture will thicken as it comes to
the boil. Serve hot with plain boiled rice.

An old-fashioned yet delicious
way of serving chicken

Chicken Pudding

Ingredients

1 chicken, skinned and boned, cut in large pieces

plain flour, for coating

butter, for frying

450ml (16fl oz) hot chicken stock

salt and pepper

1 tablespoon chopped fresh tarragon

1 tablespoon chopped fresh parsley

100g (3½oz) cooked ham, cut in strips

100g (3½oz) button mushrooms, wiped and chopped

Suet crust

100g (3½oz) fresh white breadcrumbs

200g (7oz) self-raising flour

½ teaspoon salt

1 teaspoon grated lemon zest

115g (4oz) shredded suet

SERVES 4-6 **Savoury puddings were a traditional feature of the cookery of Sussex and Kent during the nineteenth century. Fillings included mutton and oysters as well as this delicious chicken and ham recipe from Staplehurst in Kent.**

1 Coat the chicken pieces with the flour. Melt the butter in a large frying pan and add the chicken. Fry gently, turning from time to time, until golden brown all over. Add the stock, cover and simmer gently for 40 minutes, then allow to cool slightly. Season with salt and add the pepper, tarragon and parsley.

2 Meanwhile, make the suet pastry by combining the breadcrumbs, flour, salt, lemon zest and suet. Add enough water to make a coherent dough and use to line a 1.2 litre (2 pint) pudding basin (see page 82). Lift the chicken out of the cooking liquid and layer with the ham and mushrooms in the lined basin. Pour the cooking liquid over the meat and cover with a pastry lid.

3 Take a large double piece of foil or greaseproof paper, make a generous pleat in the middle and cover the top of the basin with it, remembering that the pudding will expand a little as it cooks. Tie a piece of string round the rim of the basin to hold the foil in place, and then take the string across the top of the basin to make a handle.

4 Lower the covered pudding into a large saucepan of boiling water to come halfway up the sides, and cook steadily for 1½ hours, adding more boiling water if it shows signs of boiling dry. Pin a napkin round the basin when you serve it.

Basic Roast Chicken

SERVES 4-5 **Everybody loves a roast chicken, but for the best results use the best-quality free-range bird that you can find – organic ones are usually good.**

1 Put the lemon into the body cavity of the bird, along with the herbs. Bard the breast with bacon or spread a little butter on it. Spread a little butter over a roasting tin and put the bird in on its side. Cover with a piece of oiled or buttered foil.

2 Roast in a hot preheated oven at 200°C, 400°F, Gas mark 6 for about 20 minutes, then reduce the heat to 180°C, 350°F, Gas mark 4. After 10 minutes, turn the bird on to the other side; cover and roast for another 15–20 minutes, then turn it on to its back. Add the white wine or water, then cover and return to the oven for another 30 minutes.

3 Remove the foil, baste the bird with the cooking juices and sprinkle ½ teaspoon salt over the skin. Return, uncovered, to the oven for 20 minutes. Baste once or twice more with the cooking juices – this helps to produce a really crisp, tasty skin.

4 The bird is done when the juices from the thickest part of the leg run clear (pierce it with a clean skewer or the tip of a sharp knife) – there should be no trace of pink. If there is, return the bird to the oven for a few minutes.

5 Put the chicken on a warm serving plate. Pour all the juices into a bowl, deglaze the tin with a little stock and the rest of the juices. Return to the heat, add 2 tablespoons of fat from the the cooking juices and stir in the flour. Cook gently until it turns a nutty brown. Stir in some giblet stock and season to taste.

Ingredients

1 lemon, halved

1 chicken, weighing 2kg (4½lb)

few sprigs of fresh herbs, e.g. parsley, thyme or marjoram

2 unsmoked bacon rashers

butter

3–4 tablespoons white wine or water

salt and pepper

stock from the giblets or other chicken stock

scant 1 tablespoon plain flour

Roast Chicken with Tarragon

Ingredients

a small bunch of fresh tarragon

65g (2½oz) unsalted butter

1 teaspoon grated lemon zest (preferably unwaxed), plus ½ the lemon

1 chicken, weighing 2kg (4½lb)

4 rashers streaky bacon

salt and pepper

100ml (3½fl oz) white wine or chicken stock

generous 1 teaspoon plain flour

150ml (5fl oz) single cream

SERVES 4-5 **The fresh, grassy and slightly aniseed note of tarragon is a classic partner for chicken in French cookery, with many variations on the theme, using poached or roast chicken, served hot or cold. Although recipes for the dish have appeared in several English cookery books over the last 100 years or so, it never seems to have become really popular, perhaps because French tarragon is not especially easy to grow in Britain (Russian tarragon, much more vigorous, lacks the flavour of the French variety).**

1 Pick the leaves off the tarragon and chop them. Mix a generous tablespoonful of chopped leaves with most of the butter – leave about 15g (½oz) for finishing the sauce. Put the tarragon butter and the ½ lemon inside the bird, and place the bacon rashers over the top of the chicken.

2 Roast the chicken as in the basic method given on page 105, basting from time to time with the cooking juices, turning it on to its back after 45 minutes and seasoning with salt and pepper towards the end of cooking.

3 When the bird is cooked, remove it to a warmed plate and pour all the juices into a bowl. Deglaze the tin with the white wine, making sure it bubbles fiercely, or with a little chicken stock. Pour all the herby, buttery juices back into the roasting tin. Add the lemon zest and the remaining butter worked together with the flour. Stir well, then add the cream and the rest of the chopped tarragon and heat until the sauce boils and thickens. Serve with the carved roast chicken.

Chicken in Hocchee

Ingredients

4 chicken breasts, skinned and boned

115g (4oz) green seedless grapes

1 garlic clove

2 tablespoons mixed chopped fresh parsley and sage

300ml (½ pint) chicken stock

1 small glass white wine

½ teaspoon caster sugar

½ teaspoon ground cinnamon

chopped fresh parsley, to garnish

a few extra grapes, to garnish

SERVES 4 **This is a modern adaptation of a medieval or Tudor recipe: 'Take chykens and scald them, take parsel and sawge, without any other erbes, take garlec and grapes, and stoppe the chikens ful, and seeth them in good broth, so that they may esly be boyled thereine. Messe them and cast thereto powdor-douce [a mixture of mild spices].' Try this simple dish and see for yourself how good it is.**

1 Using a sharp knife, cut a deep, horizontal pocket in each chicken breast. Mix the grapes with the garlic and herbs and stuff the chicken breasts with this mixture. Pin each breast into a neat parcel with a cocktail stick and place in a pan that just holds them. Add the stock and wine and cover the pan with some foil.

2 Bring to a simmer, then simmer gently until the chicken is cooked and tender (about 45 minutes). Remove the breasts and place them on a warm serving dish. Mix together the sugar and cinnamon and sprinkle over the chicken, then garnish with chopped parsley and grapes. Serve in a pool of cooking juices. Steamed broccoli goes well with this dish.

A delicately flavoured dish of chicken and grapes

Chicken in Red Wine

SERVES 4-6 **This is reminiscent of rich, meaty eighteenth-century ragoos. A good free-range chicken and careful preparation and seasoning gives a delicious stew, and is always well worth the effort.**

Ingredients

150g (5oz) fat bacon or pancetta, cut into 1cm (½in) dice

16 small shallots or button onions, peeled

250g (9oz) mushrooms (small open ones with dark gills are best)

about 20g (¾oz) butter

1 chicken, weighing about 2kg (4lb), cut into 8 joints

1 medium onion, chopped

1 medium carrot, chopped

4 garlic cloves, crushed

100ml (3½fl oz) brandy

1 bottle red wine (Burgundy for preference)

1 bay leaf

3–4 sprigs fresh thyme

1 teaspoon concentrated beef stock

salt and pepper

1 Fry the bacon or pancetta until crisp. Remove with a slotted spoon and put to one side. Fry the shallots or button onions in the fat until they colour, then add to the bacon. Fry the mushrooms until the tops turn gold in patches and add to the bacon and onions. Add the butter to the remaining bacon fat and fry the chicken, skin-side down, until golden. Set aside.

2 Add the chopped onion, carrot and garlic to the fat in the pan and cook briskly, stirring frequently, until the onion begins to turn gold. Warm the brandy in a ladle, ignite it and pour it into the pan, stirring well. When the flames die down, add the red wine. Add the bay leaf, thyme and beef stock and bring to the boil, then cook rapidly until reduced by half.

3 Remove the herbs, allow the sauce to cool a little and blitz it to a purée in a blender or food processor. Transfer it to a casserole. Add the chicken pieces, mushrooms, onion and bacon, a good pinch of salt and a generous grind of black pepper.

4 Cook in a preheated moderately hot oven at 180°C, 350°F, Gas mark 4 for 40 minutes, stirring halfway through. At the end of the cooking time, check that the thickest parts of the chicken are fully cooked (if they are still a bit pink, cook for a few more minutes). Taste, adding more salt if desired. A bowl of pasta, with a knob of butter and a tablespoon of finely chopped parsley stirred through, makes a good accompaniment to this dish.

Chicken with Prunes and Saffron Broth

Ingredients

12 ready-to-eat prunes

2 tablespoons whisky (optional)

400ml (14fl oz) strong chicken stock

12 whole peppercorns

a pinch of saffron threads

1 sprig fresh parsley

1 chicken, weighing about 1.5–2kg (3½–4½lb), cut into 4 joints

1 teaspoon salt

SERVES 4

This simple but well-flavoured light stew is based loosely on the Scottish cock-a-leekie, which involves a chicken and a piece of beef cooked in broth with prunes and leeks. Use a good-quality chicken; this can be cooked whole in the broth and carved afterwards if desired, but it is much easier to handle if you cut it into joints before cooking.

1 The evening before you want to make the stew, put the prunes in a small bowl with the whisky and turn them around in it. If you don't want to use any whisky, just omit this step and then proceed as below.

2 When ready to cook, put the stock in a large pan and add the prunes together with any whisky they haven't soaked up, the peppercorns, saffron and parsley. Bring to a simmer, add the chicken pieces, season with the salt and cover the pan. Simmer gently for 30–40 minutes, or until the chicken pieces are cooked all the way through.

3 Serve each joint in a deep plate, adding a generous amount of broth and two or three prunes to each helping. Boiled floury potatoes, or potatoes mashed with cooked leeks, are good accompaniments to the stew.

This is based loosely on the Scottish cock-a-leekie

Chicken and Asparagus Fricassée

Ingredients

grated zest and juice of 1 lemon

leaves of 4–6 large sprigs thyme

1 tablespoon chopped fresh parsley

salt and pepper

1 chicken, weighing about 1.5kg (3½lb), jointed and skinned

30g (1oz) butter

1 small onion, finely chopped

1 generous tablespoon plain flour

250ml (9fl oz) good chicken stock

2 bunches asparagus, washed, the woody ends of the stems discarded and the rest cut into pieces about 2cm (¾in) long

85ml (3fl oz) single cream

SERVES 4

Fricassée used to be a very popular dish and it referred to poultry and vegetables that were sautéed in butter and stewed in stock before being served in a creamy white sauce. If wished, you can garnish this with triangles of golden fried bread.

1 Mix together the lemon zest and juice, thyme and parsley. Grind in a generous amount of black pepper. Put the chicken into this mixture, turn it to coat well, then cover and leave to marinate for at least 2 hours (overnight if possible). Stir the meat around in the marinade from time to time.

2 To start the fricassée off, melt the butter in a frying pan and cook the onion gently until translucent. Lift it out and put it into a flameproof casserole or large pan. Remove the chicken from the marinade (reserve any remaining juices). Dust the joints with flour and brown them lightly in the butter used for frying the onion. Add them to the casserole or pan.

3 Add any remaining flour to the frying pan, stir well to mop up any fat, and add about two-thirds of the stock and any leftover marinade. Stir well, scraping up any residues from frying and bring to the boil. Season with ½ teaspoon salt and pour over the chicken. Cover and simmer over a low heat for 1 hour, or until the chicken pieces are cooked through. If it seems to be drying up, add a little more stock, but don't overdo it.

4 Allow the stew to cool a little and skim off any excess fat. Then add the asparagus and return to the heat for 5–10 minutes, until the asparagus is just cooked. Add the cream, stir gently and heat through. Taste, adjust the seasoning and serve with new potatoes or rice.

Old-fashioned Chicken Pie

Ingredients

2 chickens, skinned, jointed and boned (use the carcass and skin to make stock, a little of which is needed for the pie)

salt, pepper and grated nutmeg

flour, for dusting

1 large bunch fresh parsley, stems picked off, chopped

4 shallots, finely chopped

100g (3½oz) cooked ham or bacon, diced

250ml (9fl oz) chicken stock

900g (2lb) shortcrust pastry (see page 298)

plain flour, for dusting

250ml (9fl oz) double cream

SERVES 8 **Until quite recently, most farms and country smallholders kept a few hens. They scratched around the barnyard, looking for seeds, grains and insects. Versions of this dish, which is delicious hot or cold, were recorded in both Devon and Cornwall. You can ask your butcher to joint the chicken for you.**

1 Season the chicken with salt, pepper and a scrape of nutmeg. Dust with flour. Put a layer of parsley and some shallot in a large deep pie dish, and add some of the chicken pieces. Scatter the ham or bacon and the remaining parsley and shallot over the top, then fill up the dish with the remaining chicken.

2 Insert a pie funnel in the middle. Add the stock to fill the dish to the halfway mark. Roll out the pastry on a lightly floured surface and use to cover the pie. Make a hole in the centre to accommodate the pie funnel, and a pastry rose to cover it.

3 Bake in a preheated very hot oven at 220°C, 425°F, Gas mark 7 for 20 minutes, then reduce the heat to 170–180°C, 325–350°F, Gas mark 3–4 and cook for another 1–1¼ hours. At the end of the cooking time, heat the cream to boiling. Ease off the pastry rose and pour the cream into the pie.

4 Serve the pie very hot, or allow to go completely cold and then chill in the refrigerator until required.

Sautéed Turkey Escalopes with Lemon and Thyme

SERVES 4 **Lemon zest and thyme are the traditional flavourings for many meat stuffings in English cookery; they work well in this coating for escalopes. You could also make this recipe with chicken, veal or even pork escalopes, depending on what's available.**

1 Mix the thyme, lemon zest, seasoning and breadcrumbs. Break the egg into a wide bowl and beat lightly.

2 Dip both sides of each turkey escalope into the beaten egg and then coat with the breadcrumb mixture.

3 Heat a little butter in a large frying pan and fry the escalopes gently for 3–4 minutes on each side. You may have to do this in batches – keep the cooked escalopes warm in a low oven while you fry the remaining ones. Serve with lemon quarters to squeeze over, and watercress or a green salad.

Ingredients

2 teaspoons chopped fresh thyme

2 teaspoons finely grated lemon zest

salt and pepper

115g (4oz) fresh white breadcrumbs

1 egg

4 turkey escalopes, each weighing 85–100g (3–3½oz)

butter, for frying

lemon quarters and watercress or a green salad, to serve

Lemon zest and thyme are traditional flavourings

Chicken, Ham and Leek Pie

Ingredients

55g (2oz) plain flour, plus extra for dusting

salt and pepper

a pinch of grated nutmeg

1 chicken, weighing about 1.5kg (3½lb), jointed and skinned

55g (2oz) butter

about 200g (7oz) lean ham or gammon, cut in 1cm (½in) cubes

4–6 leeks (depending on size), white part only, trimmed, washed and cut in 1cm (½in) lengths

300ml (½ pint) chicken stock

1 quantity puff pastry (see page 300)

beaten egg, cream or milk, to glaze

SERVES 4

Chicken makes an excellent pie filling. In the best traditions of the English kitchen, it is often combined with ham, as is veal, while mushrooms are another common addition. Leeks are more unusual, but they make a good winter pie.

1 Season the flour with ½ teaspoon salt, some pepper and a good scrape of grated nutmeg. Dust the chicken joints with the mixture. Melt the butter in a large frying pan and brown the chicken lightly. Put the ham or gammon in the bottom of a large pie dish. Put the chicken on top, and then the sliced leeks.

2 Stir any remaining flour into the butter left in the pan, then stir in the chicken stock. Bring to the boil, stirring all the time, and cook for a few minutes. Taste to check the seasoning and add a little more if necessary. Pour this into the pie dish. Allow to cool a little.

3 Roll out the pastry on a lightly floured surface and use to cover the pie. Knock up the sides and decorate with pastry leaves made from the trimmings. Glaze with egg, cream or milk.

4 Bake in a preheated hot oven at 220°C, 425°F, Gas mark 7 for 20 minutes, then reduce the heat to 180°C, 350°F, Gas mark 4 and cook for a further 45–50 minutes, until the pastry is golden and the filling cooked through.

Braised Turkey and Celery with Tarragon Dumplings

SERVES 4

The combination of turkey and celery is a neglected classic of the English kitchen. Maybe this is because nineteenth-century versions requiring a whole boiled turkey and a sauce based on several heads of celery look daunting, but the combination still works well albeit in a less grand manner.

Ingredients

20g (¾oz) butter

4 small shallots, finely chopped

400–500g (14oz–1lb 2oz) turkey thigh, diced

20g (¾oz) flour

2–3 sprigs lemon thyme

grated zest of ½ lemon

½ teaspoon ground mace

400ml (14fl oz) turkey stock

salt and pepper

½ head celery, trimmed and cut in 2cm (¾in) lengths

Tarragon dumplings

115g (4oz) plain flour, plus a little for dusting

90g (3¼oz) fresh white breadcrumbs

1 teaspoon baking powder

a generous pinch of salt

100g (3½oz) shredded suet

1 tablespoon chopped fresh tarragon

1 Melt the butter in a heavy frying pan. Add the shallots and cook gently for about 10 minutes, or until translucent. Toss the turkey meat in the flour and fry gently until lightly coloured. Add the thyme, lemon zest and mace, then stir in the stock. Season with 1 scant teaspoon salt and a little pepper and add the celery. Bring to a simmer, then transfer to a casserole and cover with a lid.

2 Cook in a preheated moderately slow oven at 170°C, 325°F, Gas mark 3 for about 1 hour, until the meat is just cooked but not yet tender. Skim off any excess fat.

3 Meanwhile, make the dumplings: put everything except the water in a bowl and mix well. Add about 200ml (7fl oz) water gradually, stirring until it forms a soft, slightly sticky dough (add a little more water if necessary). Dust a board and your fingers with flour and form the dough into 20 dumplings.

4 Put the dumplings on top of the stew and return to the oven, uncovered, for another 20–30 minutes, or until they are crisp on top and golden.

Daube of Turkey

Ingredients

4 turkey breast steaks, weighing 100–125g (3½–4½oz) each

4 thin rashers of bacon

100g (3½oz) pork rind, cut in small pieces

1 medium onion, finely chopped

4–6 small shallots, finely chopped

1 medium carrot, diced

1 beef tomato, skinned, deseeded and diced

1 garlic clove , crushed

100g (3½oz) chorizo sausage, cut in thick slices

a bouquet garni of 1 piece of leek, celery, 1 bay leaf, a few sprigs fresh thyme and parsley and a strip of orange zest

½ teaspoon salt

pepper

400ml (14fl oz) white wine

SERVES 4 **Daube is a term now applied to a dish of slowly braised meat and vegetables. Ask the butcher for a piece of pork rind – it's not essential but it will add body and richness to the sauce. Chorizo is not traditional, but it goes well with the turkey.**

1 Wrap each piece of turkey in a rasher of bacon. Blanch the pork rind by putting it in a small pan, adding boiling water and cooking for 2–3 minutes, then drain. Mix the onion, shallots, carrot, tomato and garlic together.

2 Put the pork rind into an ovenproof dish and add a layer of vegetables. Put the chorizo on top and add some more vegetables. Put the turkey steaks on top of this and add the bouquet garni. Season with the salt and some pepper (the sausage and bacon will also be salty, so be cautious). Cover with the remaining vegetables and pour in the white wine.

3 Cover the dish with a lid with a layer of foil underneath to make it airtight. Transfer to a preheated low oven at 140°C, 275°F, Gas mark 1 and cook for 2½–3 hours.

4 This daube can be eaten hot or allowed to cool in the dish and gently re-heated when required. If the sauce seems a bit thin, just pour some into a small pan and reduce by fast boiling before returning it to the stew.

A daube is a dish of slowly braised meat and vegetables

Roast Goose with Sage and Onion

Ingredients

1 goose with giblets, weighing about 4.5kg (10lb)

salt

Sage and onion stuffing

1 large onion, finely chopped

85g (3oz) sage leaves, finely chopped

300g (10½oz) fresh white breadcrumbs

1 teaspoon salt

grated zest of ½ lemon

generous amount of pepper

1 egg, beaten

Gravy

2 rashers bacon, cut in strips

½ onion, chopped

1 carrot, chopped

2 celery sticks, chopped

goose giblets, excluding the liver

1 bay leaf

70ml (2½fl oz) brandy

1 heaped teaspoon cornflour

salt and pepper

SERVES 6 **At Saltash, on the banks of the River Tamar in Cornwall, Mr and Mrs Hunn rear geese and turkeys for Christmas. The recipe given here is the classic English way with geese. Ask your butcher to retain the giblets, but exclude the liver when making gravy. Fry it in butter, whizz up in a blender and season for a little pâté to eat while the bird roasts.**

1 To make the stuffing, mix the onion, sage and breadcrumbs. Add the salt and lemon zest and grind in plenty of pepper. Use the egg to bind the mixture. Remove any visible lumps of fat from inside the goose (render them down for roasting potatoes) and spoon in the stuffing.

2 Put the goose on a wire rack in a large roasting tin and rub the skin with salt. Roast in a preheated hot oven at 200°C, 400°F, Gas mark 6 for 2½–3 hours, occasionally pouring off the fat in the roasting tin.

3 To make the stock for the gravy, cook the bacon gently until the fat runs. Add the vegetables and the giblets and cook until browned, then add the bay leaf, cover with water and leave to simmer gently, allowing the liquid to reduce by about a third to make a well-flavoured giblet stock.

4 When the goose is cooked, remove from the oven and place on a warm plate, then leave to rest. Pour off the fat from the roasting tin. Add the brandy and let it bubble, scraping up any sediment. Strain in the stock from the giblets and bring to the boil. Taste and adjust the seasoning. Mix the cornflour with a little water and stir into the gravy, heating again until the mixture thickens. Serve the gravy separately with the carved roast goose.

Slow-roasted Duck Legs with Marmalade

SERVES 4 **The delicious orange flavourings in this recipe can also be used to marinate portions of duck before roasting or sautéeing them.**

1 Put the duck legs in an ovenproof dish that holds them neatly. Mix the marmalade, orange and lemon juices and pour over the duck. Cover and leave in the refrigerator to marinate for 24 hours. Stir from time to time to make sure the legs are well coated with the marinade.

2 Cook the duck legs in a preheated cool oven at 140°C, 275°F, Gas mark 1 for 1¾ hours, turning them after 1 hour. About 15 minutes before the end of cooking time, pour the fat and cooking juices into a bowl and turn the oven up to 170°C, 325°F, Gas mark 3 to crisp the skin.

3 When the duck legs are ready, remove them to a serving plate. Skim the fat off the reserved cooking juices and use them to deglaze the roasting dish (you may want to add a little stock or water to help the process along, but don't overdo it – there should be a relatively small quantity of thin, concentrated gravy). Taste, adjust the seasoning and serve. A salad of crisp watercress and rocket and fried potatoes go well with this dish.

Ingredients

4 duck legs

1 generous tablespoon bitter orange marmalade

juice of 1 (sweet) orange

juice of 1 lemon

a little stock (optional)

salt and pepper

Marmalade adds a bitter twist to the orange flavouring

Stewed Duck with Green Peas

Ingredients

30g (1oz) butter

1 duck, jointed, or 4 duck joints

flour, for dusting

100g (3½oz) pancetta or bacon, cut in matchsticks

8 small shallots, halved

2 tablespoons brandy

a bouquet garni of fresh parsley, thyme, 1 bay leaf and 1 sprig mint

zest of ½ lemon, cut in thin strips

salt

3–4 cloves, pounded to a powder

a pinch of cayenne

345ml (12fl oz) well-flavoured beef stock

200g (7oz) frozen peas

4–6 spring onions, finely sliced

leaves from 6–8 sprigs fresh mint, finely chopped

leaves from 6–8 sprigs fresh basil, torn into shreds

SERVES 4

Recorded from the early eighteenth century onwards, stewed duck and green peas became a classic of English summer food. Success depends on good stock, which must be well flavoured. If in doubt about this, start with about half as much again, then add onion, carrot, parsley and mushroom trimmings and allow it to reduce gently to the amount required. Beef stock or gravy was always specified for this dish.

1 Melt the butter in a wide frying pan. Dust the duck joints with flour, then brown slowly on both sides in the butter. Remove from the pan and pour off the fat.

2 Return the pan to a low heat. Spread the pancetta or bacon and shallots over the bottom. Put the duck on top, then pour in the brandy and let it bubble. Add the bouquet garni, lemon zest, 1 scant teaspoon salt, the cloves and cayenne. Pour in the stock, bring to a simmer and cover. Let the mixture stew very gently for about 1 hour. Towards the end of this time, test the duck meat to see if it is cooked – the juices should run clear. When done, transfer the pieces to a serving dish and keep warm. Discard the bouquet garni. Skim off the excess fat.

3 Return the pan with the cooking juices to the heat. Add the peas and spring onions and bring to the boil. Season if necessary. As soon as the peas are done, remove from the heat, stir in the mint and basil and pour into deep serving plates. Arrange the duck on top and serve with little new potatoes.

Game Casserole

SERVES 4

This is one of the staples of the country kitchen and a delicious way of using up leftover meat from the carcasses of game birds, such as pheasant and partridge, as well as venison, rabbit and hare.

Ingredients

400–500g (14oz–1lb 2oz) meat cut from game birds and animals

2 tablespoons duck or goose fat, beef dripping or lard

1 medium onion, chopped

1 celery stick, chopped

1 medium carrot, chopped

2 garlic cloves, crushed

1 teaspoon ground coriander

a bouquet garni of 1 bay leaf, thyme, marjoram, parsley sprigs and a few strips of orange zest

200ml (7fl oz) red wine

7.5g (¼oz) dried porcini

200ml (7fl oz) boiling water

55g (2oz) bacon or pancetta, cut in small dice

salt and pepper

1 tablespoon balsamic vinegar (optional)

1 Cut the meat as neatly as possible into 2.5cm (1in) cubes. Heat the fat in a frying pan and add the onion, celery and carrot. Fry briskly, turning often, until they begin to turn slightly golden. Add the garlic, coriander and bouquet garni and pour in the wine. Simmer gently for 10–15 minutes, making sure that not too much liquid evaporates. Pour everything into a large bowl and allow to cool, then add the meat. Turn well in the mixture, cover and leave in a cold place to marinate overnight.

2 The following day, wash the dried porcini and put them in a small bowl. Pour the boiling water over them and set aside for at least 30 minutes to infuse and swell up.

3 Tip the meat into a strainer over a bowl. Keep the marinade that drips through and the bouquet garni. Heat a flameproof casserole and fry the bacon or pancetta until it has yielded most of its fat. Remove and keep to one side. Blot any excess liquid off the meat, then fry it in the bacon fat. When the pieces are browned, remove from the pan. Pour in the reserved marinade and bring to the boil, then strain and return to the pan. Add the bouquet garni, the porcini and their soaking liquid, all the meat, and salt and pepper to taste, then return to a simmer.

4 Cover with greaseproof paper or foil and the lid of the casserole. Cook in a preheated low oven at 150°C, 300°F, Gas mark 2 for about 1½ hours, or until the meat is cooked. Stir in the vinegar at the end, if using. Serve with jacket potatoes and a dish of cabbage cooked with juniper berries.

Game Pie

Ingredients

55g (2oz) butter

450g (1lb) venison, cubed

400–500g (14oz–1lb 2oz) pork sausage meat, divided into 10–12 balls

450g (1lb) assorted other game, cut off the bone, such as pheasant, pigeon, partridge, rabbit, hare

2 tablespoons plain flour

100ml (3½fl oz) red wine

300ml (½ pint) game stock

salt and pepper

grated nutmeg

450g (1lb) shortcrust pastry (see page 298)

plain flour, for dusting

beaten egg, for sealing and glazing

SERVES 10 **Game pie can be made in the same way as pork pie with hot-water crust and jellied stock, using 450g (1lb) meat from game and the same from pork. This version is a bit of a hybrid between a raised pie and a more standard short-pastry version.**

1 Take a 20cm (8in) round cake tin with a loose bottom, and line the base with greaseproof paper.

2 Melt the butter in a large frying pan. Brown the venison, sausage meat and the other game if it is raw. Remove, leaving as much fat as possible in the pan. Stir in the flour. Add the wine, scraping the bottom of the pan to pick up all the residues. Pour in the stock and simmer gently for 20 minutes. Add salt, pepper and nutmeg to taste. The sauce should be well seasoned. Turn into a basin and allow to cool to tepid.

3 Roll out three-quarters of the pastry on a lightly floured surface into a large circle. Use to line the prepared tin. Spread the pastry so it drapes over the sides. Ease it over the bottom, into the edges and up the sides. Roll out the remaining quarter for the lid. Distribute the venison over the bottom and top with the other game, then add the sausagemeat balls. Pour in the sauce. Brush the edges of the pastry with beaten egg, cover with the pastry lid and press the edges together firmly to seal.

4 Trim, crimping the edges decoratively and adding decorations of pastry flowers and leaves made from the trimmings. Glaze with beaten egg. Place on a heated baking tray and cook in a preheated very hot oven at 220°C, 425°F, Gas mark 7 for about 20–30 minutes, then turn the oven down to 170°C, 325°F, Gas mark 3 and cook for a further 1½ hours. Remove from the oven and allow to cool in the tin overnight.

Roast Pheasant

SERVES 3-4

Slices of lemon and pancetta are used to cover the pheasant breast in this recipe. The pancetta creates a thin, crisp crust round the bird. Bacon can be used instead, especially if you can buy fatty, old-fashioned dry-cured bacon cut thin on a bacon slicer.

1 Remove the skin from the pheasant. Preheat the oven to 200°C, 400°F, Gas mark 6. Peel the lemon completely by cutting off each end, standing it up like a barrel on a board and slicing the peel off in vertical strips, taking off zest, skin and pith together. Cut the lemon across in the thinnest possible slices.

2 Lay the pheasant on its back and cover the breast and as much as possible of the upper surface of the bird with the lemon slices. Then swaddle it in pancetta, overlapping the slices where necessary. Pass some string under the back of the bird about halfway down the wings, then bring it up over the breast in a cross and back under in another cross somewhere near the middle of the thighs and up again, tying it neatly.

3 Lightly butter a roasting tin and put the pheasant in on its back. Roast, checking occasionally that the pancetta isn't browning too much; if it is darkening a lot, turn the heat down slightly and roast for a little longer. After 20 minutes, reduce the heat to 180°C, 350°F, Gas mark 4 and roast for a further 20–30 minutes. It is done when a skewer is pushed into the thickest part of the leg and the juices run clear.

4 Remove the pheasant to a warmed serving dish. Pour the juices into a small bowl and skim off as much fat as possible, then return a dessertspoon of fat to the tin. Sprinkle in the flour, then stir in the juices and mix to a paste. Add the stock, bit by bit, stirring constantly and bring to the boil; you should have a thin, well-flavoured gravy. Remove the pancetta (which should be deliciously crisp) just before carving and serve with the bird.

Ingredients

1 pheasant

1 lemon

85g (3oz) pancetta, thinly sliced

unsalted butter

1 teaspoon plain flour

150ml (¼ pint) stock made from the giblets of the bird, or from chicken or veal

Pheasant with Spiced Sausage and Peppers

Ingredients

2 tablespoons butter, duck or goose fat

1 pheasant, jointed into 8 pieces

1 tablespoon plain flour, for dusting

140g (5oz) unsmoked pancetta or bacon, in one piece

12 small shallots, peeled

4 whole garlic cloves, peeled

2 tablespoons brandy

1 fresh red chilli, deseeded and finely sliced or diced (optional)

a bouquet garni of several sprigs fresh oregano, thyme, parsley and 2 strips of orange zest

200g (7oz) Spanish chorizo, cut in 1cm (½in) lengths

1 red pepper, deseeded and diced

1 yellow pepper, deseeded and diced

200ml (7fl oz) game or chicken stock

SERVES 4-6 **This recipe is old-fashioned in the sense that it is based on one first published 60 years ago, by Elizabeth David in her classic book *French Provincial Cookery* (1960). This dish is very different to standard game recipes and is well worth trying out.**

1 Melt the butter or fat in a flameproof casserole. Pat the pheasant joints dry, then shake the flour over them. Brown them quickly all over in the fat, then remove and set aside.

2 Cut the pancetta or bacon into dice, about 1cm (½in) square, and add them to the fat. Cook fairly briskly, stirring from time to time, until the fat is translucent. Add the shallots and continue to cook, stirring, so that they start to brown in places. Stir in the garlic and cook a moment longer.

3 Warm the brandy in a ladle, let it catch light and pour over the bacon mixture. Shake the dish until the flames die down, then return the pheasant to the pan. Add the chilli, if using, and the bouquet garni. Put the chorizo on top and then add the peppers. Pour in the stock.

4 Cover the casserole tightly and simmer over a very low heat for about 1 hour, or cook in a preheated slow oven at 170°C, 325°F, Gas mark 3 for 1–1½ hours. At the end of cooking time, uncover, stir well and taste. The bacon and sausage should have given enough salt to the sauce. Serve with plain boiled rice.

Venison Casseroled with Apricots

Ingredients

55g (2oz) dried apricots

85g (3oz) butter

2 medium onions, sliced

450g (1lb) venison, cut in large cubes

2 tablespoons plain flour

2 teaspoons crushed juniper berries

salt and pepper

300ml (½ pint) apple or apricot juice

300ml (½ pint) red wine

chopped fresh parsley, to garnish

a bowl of Greek yoghurt, to serve

SERVES 4

The Romans first fenced game parks in Britain to raise and hunt deer and wild boar. Venison has been prized as a meat ever since.

1 Soak the apricots in cold water overnight. Preheat the oven to 170°C, 325°F, Gas mark 3.

2 In a sauté pan, melt the butter and sauté the onions until soft and golden. Take out with a slotted spoon and place in a casserole dish. Now sauté the venison until brown and add to the onions with any cooking juices from the sauté pan. Mix the flour with the crushed juniper berries and salt and pepper to taste. Sprinkle over the meat and onions and turn them well in the flour mixture.

3 Place the casserole in the oven for 10 minutes to cook the flour. Meanwhile, heat the juice and wine gently in a pan. Remove the casserole from the oven and add the juice, wine and soaked apricots. Stir and return to the oven.

4 Cook gently for at least 2 hours, or until the meat is tender. This may take longer if the venison was wild rather than farmed. To serve, sprinkle with parsley and hand round a bowl of yoghurt separately for guests to add if they wish.

The apricots add sweetness to this rich game dish

Pot-roasted Shoulder of Venison

Ingredients

6–8 black peppercorns

3 whole cloves

½ teaspoon grated nutmeg

1 thick slice fat bacon or pancetta, 115g (4oz), cut in strips or lardons

1 boned shoulder of venison, weighing about 1kg (2lb 3oz) in a flat piece

250ml (9fl oz) dry white wine

4 bay leaves, bruised

a bouquet garni of 2 sprigs each fresh marjoram, thyme and rosemary, 1 slice of lemon and a few bruised juniper berries

2 tablespoons vegetable oil or beef dripping

2 carrots, cut in chunks

¼ turnip, cut in chunks

½ onion, cut in 4 chunks

15g (½oz) butter, blended to a paste with 15g (½oz) plain flour

1 tablespoon capers, rinsed and roughly chopped

salt

SERVES 6-8 **A good dish for a chilly winter's day, this recipe is adapted from one in Martha Bradley's *The British Housewife*, first published in 1756.**

1 Grind the peppercorns and cloves together and mix with the nutmeg. Spread this spice mixture on a plate and roll the lardons in it, until well coated. Make small incisions in the meat and push the lardons into them, so they lie just below the surface. Roll and tie the venison into a neat shape.

2 Put the white wine and bay leaves in a large dish or casserole and add the venison and bouquet garni. Leave to marinate for about 3 hours, turning from time to time.

3 Preheat the oven to 140°C, 275°F, Gas mark 1. Heat the oil or dripping in a flameproof casserole. Fry the carrot, turnip and onion briskly until they brown in places. Add the marinade and bring to the boil. Turn off the heat, add the venison and bouquet garni and cover the dish. Cook in the oven for 3 hours, turning the meat every hour or so, until really tender.

4 Lift out the venison and transfer it to a warm serving plate. Remove and discard the vegetables and bouquet garni. Set the casserole containing the cooking juices over a high heat and boil rapidly until the juices are reduced to half their original volume. Off the heat, add the butter and flour paste in small pieces, shaking the pan to mix them in. The sauce should thicken a little. Stir in the capers, and check the seasoning.

5 Slice up the venison (the meat around the lardons will appear pink or red, due to saltpetre in the bacon cure leaching into the venison) and serve with the hot sauce, accompanied by redcurrant jelly and a buttery purée of potato and celeriac.

Venison and Damson Casserole

SERVES 4 The idea for this recipe came partly from a friend who cooks beef with damsons, and partly from an extension of the sweet–sour flavour of redcurrant jelly, so often used with game in the English kitchen. Damsons have a very short season of 2–3 weeks. If unavailable, substitute plums and add a little damson jam or jelly for tartness.

1 Heat half the butter in a suitable pan or flameproof casserole. Add the onion, carrot, celery and garlic. Fry briskly, turning frequently, until the volume is much reduced and the onion is starting to turn golden brown at the edges. Remove from the pan with a slotted spoon and put to one side.

2 Flour the venison. Add the remaining butter to the pan and turn the meat in it, just enough to brown it on all sides. Return the vegetables to the pan and scatter in any remaining flour, stirring well. Pour in the port and allow it to bubble. Then stir in enough water to make a sauce. Add the damsons or plums and the damson jelly, if using, the juniper berries, cloves, 1 scant teaspoon salt and some black pepper.

3 Stir well, then cover the casserole and cook in a preheated low oven at 140°C, 275°F, Gas mark 1 for about 3 hours, or until the venison is tender. Taste and correct the seasoning; if damsons alone have been used, add a little sugar to counteract their tart flavour. Good bread is the best partner for this dish.

Ingredients

55g (2oz) butter

1 medium onion, finely chopped

100g (3½oz) carrot, finely chopped

100g (3½oz) celery, finely chopped

1 garlic clove, finely chopped

1 generous tablespoon plain flour

500g (1lb 2oz) stewing venison, cut in pieces 3cm (1¼in) square

100ml (3½fl oz) port

about 300ml (½ pint) water

250g (9oz) damsons or red plums, stones removed

3 tablespoons damson jam or jelly (if using plums, not damsons)

6 juniper berries, bruised

4 cloves

salt and pepper

sugar, if needed

Venison Steaks with Allspice, Juniper Berries and Sloe Gin

Ingredients

15g (½oz) butter

1 tablespoon olive oil

4 venison steaks, each weighing about 115g (4oz)

about 4 tablespoons sloe gin

6 juniper berries, bruised

a generous pinch of ground allspice

about 120ml (4fl oz) stock (venison for preference)

4–6 tablespoons thick cream

salt and pepper

SERVES 4

In the past, venison was a highly prized food of the nobility, and deer stalking in the Scottish Highlands still has an image as an exclusive sport. But red deer are now farmed in several places, and the population of roe and fallow deer has expanded, making this low-fat, flavoursome meat easier and cheaper to buy. Juniper, an excellent flavouring, was once a common bush across much of Scotland.

1 Heat the butter and olive oil together in a heavy frying pan. Add the venison steaks and cook quickly, for 3–4 minutes on each side, depending on their thickness. Venison is best on the rare side when cooked this way; don't overdo it, or the meat will be tough. Remove to a warm serving dish and keep hot.

2 Add the sloe gin to the pan and allow to bubble, then add the juniper berries, allspice and the stock. Cook rapidly until only 3 or 4 tablespoons of liquid remain in the pan. Stir in the cream, adjust the seasoning and serve with the vension steaks. New potatoes and some French beans are good with this.

Juniper berries and sloe gin are perfect flavourings for venison

Rabbit with Cider and Dumplings

Ingredients

1 rabbit, jointed

brine (optional)

100g (3½oz) bacon, cut in lardons

about 30g (1oz) butter

1 medium onion, finely chopped

about 30g (1oz) flour

½ teaspoon salt

pepper

Marinade

400ml (14fl oz) cider

finely grated zest of 1 lemon

2 garlic cloves, chopped

8 juniper berries, bruised

a bouquet garni of several sprigs fresh parsley and thyme and 2 sprigs rosemary

Dumplings

1 quantity dumpling mixture (see page 301)

1 tablespoon chopped fresh parsley

leaves from 2–3 sprigs fresh thyme, chopped

SERVES 4-6 **This rabbit stew requires marinating overnight in an aromatic mixture. You can still buy fresh rabbit from old-fashioned country butchers, although it is also sold by many supermarket chains.**

1 Put the rabbit in a bowl and pour the brine over, if using. Leave in a cool place for a few hours, then drain, discarding the brine. Rinse the bowl and replace the pieces of rabbit. Mix the marinade ingredients thoroughly and pour over the rabbit joints. Cover and leave overnight.

2 The next day, drain the rabbit and reserve the marinade. Add the bacon to a large frying pan and let it cook gently until all the fat has run out. Remove the bacon to a dish. Add the butter and fry the onion fairly briskly until it is translucent. Remove with a slotted spoon, allowing as much fat as possible to run back into the pan. Put the onion with the bacon.

3 Pat the rabbit joints dry, dredge them with the flour and fry them in the remaining fat until lightly browned. Dust in any remaining flour and pour in the marinade. Add the bacon, onion, salt and a generous amount of black pepper, and stir well. Transfer the contents of the pan to a casserole. Cover with a lid and cook in a preheated cool oven at 140°C, 275°F, Gas mark 1 for 1½ hours.

4 Make up the dumpling mixture, incorporating the herbs, and use a spoon to drop pieces the size of a large walnut on to the top of the stew. Return the casserole to the oven, uncovered, for a further 20 minutes. Finally, turn the oven up to 180°C, 350°F, Gas mark 4 and cook for another 10 minutes to help the dumplings cook through.

Cullen Skink

Ingredients

400–500g (14oz–1lb 2oz) smoked haddock

1 small onion, thinly sliced

1 bay leaf

a few peppercorns

700g (1lb 9oz) floury potatoes, cut in 1cm (½in) cubes

salt

100ml (3½fl oz) single cream

chopped fresh chives or 2 spring onions, very finely sliced, to garnish

SERVES 4

This is a version of a traditional Scottish soup of smoked fish and potatoes. We have altered it slightly to push it closer to North American chowder-type dishes, and create something in between a soup and a stew. It makes a good light lunch or supper.

1 Put the smoked haddock, onion, bay leaf and peppercorns in a pan and cover with cold water. Heat and then simmer for about 10 minutes, or until the fish is cooked. Remove it from the pan (keep the cooking liquid).

2 When the fish has cooled enough to handle, carefully remove all the skin and bones. Flake the flesh and set on one side. Return the bones and skin to the pan, then cover with a lid and simmer gently for about 30 minutes to make a stock. Strain and measure it; 565–700ml (1–1¼ pints) will be needed. If there isn't enough, make up the quantity with water.

3 Put the stock and potatoes into a clean pan and bring to the boil. Let them simmer until the potatoes are well cooked and just starting to break up a little, giving body to the liquid. Stir in the fish and heat through. Taste and add more salt if desired; remember, the smoked fish may be quite salty. Stir in the cream.

4 Divide the soup between 4 soup bowls and scatter each portion with chopped chives or a little sliced spring onion. Serve hot with crusty wholemeal bread.

This is a variation on a North American chowder

Mock Crab

SERVES 2 **The idea of calling this pleasant supper dish 'mock crab' may have evolved during World War II, when the real thing was difficult to find away from the coast. It can be put together very quickly from ingredients that most people have readily to hand. For a vegetarian version, omit the anchovies and add a little chopped fresh basil.**

1 Put the tomatoes in a bowl, cover with boiling water and leave to stand for 1–2 minutes. Drain and peel off the skins. Cut in half and remove and discard the pips. Cut the tomato flesh into slivers or cubes.

2 Melt the butter in a pan. Add the onion and tomatoes and stew very gently over a low heat for about 5 minutes, until the onion is soft and translucent. Stir in the cheese.

3 Beat the eggs together in a small bowl, then mix in the breadcrumbs. Stir this into the tomato mixture, together with the anchovies, if using, and continue to cook very gently, stirring all the time, until the eggs thicken.

4 Remove the pan from the heat and season to taste. Serve immediately with some toast or good crusty bread, or allow to cool and use as a sandwich filling.

Ingredients

2–3 large, well-flavoured tomatoes, about 200g (7oz) in total

55g (2oz) butter

1 small onion, very finely chopped

40g (1½oz) strong Cheddar cheese, finely grated

2 eggs

2 tablespoons fresh white breadcrumbs

4–6 anchovy fillets, chopped into small pieces (optional)

salt and pepper

toast or crusty bread, to serve

Salmon in Pastry

Ingredients

40g (1½oz) butter, softened

grated zest of ½ lemon

grated zest of ½ orange

2.5–4cm (1–1½in) piece fresh root ginger, peeled and finely grated

½ teaspoon black peppercorns, coarsely ground

½ teaspoon finely grated nutmeg

1 piece of skinned salmon fillet, weighing about 565g (1¼lb)

½ teaspoon salt

55g (2oz) raisins

plain flour, for dusting

225g (8oz) frozen puff pastry, thawed

1 egg, beaten, to seal and glaze

SERVES 4

Pastry was often served as a covering for a whole fish, or part of one, to protect it from drying out or scorching when cooked in the fierce heat of a brick oven. Like kitchen foil, it also helps to preserve the flavours of any seasonings or stuffing. The one used here is based on a seventeenth-century recipe. It is best to use the tail end of a salmon, as it is least likely to contain lots of small bones.

1 Preheat the oven to 220°C, 425°F, Gas mark 7. Blend the butter, lemon and orange zest, ginger, ground peppercorns and nutmeg together in a small bowl. Take the piece of salmon and cut it in half lengthways. Season each half with the salt, then spread the butter mixture over the top of one piece and scatter the raisins over it. Cover with the other piece of salmon.

2 On a lightly floured work surface, roll out the pastry into an oblong slightly longer than the salmon and twice as wide, to a thickness of approximately 3mm (⅛in). Put the stuffed salmon on top and roll the pastry around it, so that the fish is completely enclosed. Trim off and reserve any surplus pastry to make a neat parcel. Brush the edges of the pastry with some of the beaten egg and press firmly together to seal. Turn the parcel over so that the join in the pastry is underneath, and then use the leftover pastry trimmings to decorate the top. Brush the pastry with the remaining beaten egg to glaze, then lay the parcel on a sheet of baking paper on a baking tray.

3 Cook in the preheated hot oven for 15 minutes. Lower the heat to 180°C, 350°F, Gas mark 4 and cook for a further 15 minutes. Serve hot, warm or cold.

Stewed Soles

Ingredients

2 small soles, each weighing about 250g (9oz)

120ml (4fl oz) white wine

a few peppercorns

1 blade of mace

1 strip of lemon zest, about 3cm (1¼in) long

100g (3½oz) shelled prawns

salt

1 generous teaspoon butter

1 generous teaspoon plain flour

1 tablespoon finely chopped fresh parsley

lemon wedges, to serve (optional)

SERVES 2 **This recipe is based on one that appears in an early Scottish cookery book by Elizabeth Cleland: *A New and Easy Method of Cookery* (1755). A simple method for cooking soles or any other flat fish, it needs a wide shallow pan in which they will fit in a single layer. Ask the fishmonger to remove the skins from the soles.**

1 Put the soles side by side in a shallow pan and pour the wine over them. Add the peppercorns, mace and lemon zest, and a good pinch of salt. Bring to a simmer, then cover (use foil if the pan doesn't have a lid) and cook over a low heat for 10 minutes. By this time, the fish should be cooked through, although the upper side might not be quite done – the best way to deal with this is to put the pan under a hot grill for 2–3 minutes. Add a little water if the cooking liquid shows signs of evaporating – there should be about the same amount as at the start.

2 When the soles are cooked, remove them to warmed plates. Put the pan with the cooking liquid back over a low heat. Remove the spices and lemon zest and add the prawns. Allow them to heat through to boiling. Knead the butter and flour and dot over the surface of the liquid, shaking the pan so that it disperses and thickens the sauce. Stir and pour over the fish.

3 Sprinkle the soles with a little parsley, and serve immediately, garnished with lemon wedges, if you like.

A simple method for cooking soles

Smoked Haddock and New Potato Salad

Ingredients

about 310g (11oz) undyed smoked haddock or 2 Arbroath smokies

about 300ml (½ pint) milk (if using cold-smoked haddock)

400g (14oz) new potatoes

½ bunch of spring onions, trimmed

1 tablespoon lemon juice

3 tablespoons olive oil

salt and pepper

chopped fresh parsley, to garnish

SERVES 4 **Fish smoking was particularly associated with the Scottish coast from Fife northwards to Aberdeen. If you can buy the little smoked haddocks known as Arbroath smokies, they are good in this dish, and need no preliminary cooking, as the process uses hot smoke, which cooks the fish.**

1 If using cold-smoked haddock, put the fish in a shallow ovenproof dish and cover with the milk. Cook in a preheated oven at 190°C, 375°F, Gas mark 5 for 15–20 minutes, until the fish is opaque and flakes away from the skin easily.

2 Drain and allow to cool a little, then remove and discard all the skin and flake the flesh. Take care to remove all the bones as you do this. If using smokies, cooking is unnecessary, but the skin and bones will still have to be removed.

3 Cover the potatoes with water in a pan and cook until tender. Drain and cut them into quarters if very small, or large cubes if bigger. Cut the spring onions obliquely in fine slices and mix with the potatoes while they are still warm.

4 Make a dressing using the lemon juice and olive oil, and seasoning it with salt and pepper. Toss the potatoes and spring onions in this, then mix in the fish. Garnish with plenty of chopped parsley and serve, just cooled.

Cornish Fish Pie

SERVES 4 **Cornish farmhouse traditions mix fish and dairy produce. The fresh wild sea bass that is used in this recipe is in season between August and March; smaller farmed fish are available all year round. Ask your fishmonger for bones and trimmings for stock.**

1 Put the fish bones and trimmings in a small pan, cover with water and simmer gently for 20 minutes to produce a little fish stock. Cut the fish fillets into slices about 3cm (1¼in) wide. Grease a large pie dish and lay the fish in it. Scatter salt, pepper and chopped parsley over the top and then add 4 tablespoons of the fish stock.

2 Roll out the pastry on a floured surface and use to cover the pie, trimming the edges neatly and sealing them. Cut a hole in the centre and make a pastry rose to cover it. Glaze the top with some beaten egg.

3 Bake the pie in a preheated very hot oven at 220°C, 425°F, Gas mark 7 for about 15 minutes. Warm the single cream gently until almost boiling. Lift the pastry rose and pour the warmed cream into the pie. Return to the oven for another 5 minutes. Just before serving, lift the crust gently at the edge and spoon the clotted cream over the fish.

Ingredients

450g (1lb) sea bass fillets, skinned; bones and trimmings reserved

a little butter, for greasing

salt and pepper

1 tablespoon chopped fresh parsley

450g (1lb) shortcrust pastry made with butter and lard mixed (see page 298)

plain flour, for dusting

beaten egg, to glaze

100ml (3½fl oz) single cream

2 tablespoons clotted cream

This is filled with sea bass in a rich, creamy sauce

Salmon Fishcakes

Ingredients

225g (8oz) salmon fillet

450g (1lb) potatoes, cooked, mashed and cooled

2 tablespoons finely chopped onion or spring onion

2 tablespoons finely chopped fresh parsley

grated zest and juice of ½ lemon

1 egg, well beaten

salt and pepper

2 tablespoons plain flour

25g (1oz) butter

2 tablespoons olive or sunflower oil

lemon wedges, to serve

tartare sauce, to serve

SERVES 4 **This is a great way to use up leftover fish if you have poached a whole salmon. The contrast between the crisp outside and the pink, cream and green inside of the cake is particularly appetising.**

1 Steam the salmon until cooked (approximately 10 minutes). Put in a mixing bowl and flake, removing any bones. Allow to cool. Then add the mashed potato, onion, parsley and lemon. Use the rest of the lemon for the lemon-wedge garnish. Stir in the beaten egg and season to taste. The mixture will be quite soft, but if you wet your hands before forming the cakes it will not stick quite so much.

2 Divide the mixture into 8 pieces. Use your hands to shape them into patties, then dust them with the flour, mixed with a little extra seasoning.

3 Heat the butter and oil in a large frying pan and fry the cakes on each side until crisp and golden. Serve immediately with lemon wedges, tartare sauce and green vegetables or a salad.

This is a great way of using up leftover salmon

Haddock, Leek and Potato Stew with Mussels

Ingredients

500–600g (1lb 2oz–1lb 5oz) haddock, skin and bones removed and reserved

a few stalks or leaves of fresh parsley

1 celery stick

2 leeks, washed, trimmed and cut in 2cm (¾in) slices (keep the trimmings)

565ml (1 pint) water

310g (11oz) mussels, scrubbed

2 large potatoes, cut in 1cm (½in) dice

1 scant teaspoon salt

pepper

55ml (2fl oz) single cream

a little fresh tarragon, chopped (optional)

SERVES 4

Onions were the usual vegetable in this stew, but leeks give a good flavour and a pretty contrast of colour. Ask the fishmonger to skin the fish for you, but get him to put the skin in the parcel, together with some fish bones if possible.

1 Gently simmer the fish skin, bones, parsley, celery and trimmings of leek with the water in a pan for 20 minutes, then strain, reserving the liquid as stock.

2 Pull the beards off the mussels, discarding any that are cracked or don't close when tapped. Put them in a pan with a tight-fitting lid and then steam over fairly high heat for a few minutes. Strain the liquor into the fish stock, and keep the mussels on one side – discard any that do not open.

3 Put the potatoes and sliced leeks in a pan or a flameproof casserole. Pour the stock over and season with the salt and a little pepper. Cook for about 10 minutes, until the potatoes are just tender. Cut the haddock into slices about 2.5cm (1in) thick, and put them on top of the vegetables. Simmer for another 5 minutes, or until the fish is just done. Add the mussels and allow them to heat through.

4 Put the vegetables and fish into soup bowls and pour the cooking liquid over them. Add a spoonful of cream to each portion and scatter with chopped tarragon, if using.

Water Souchy

Ingredients

1kg (2lb 3oz) mixed white fish, such as haddock or cod, sea bass and lemon sole

1 small onion, sliced

1 small carrot, chopped

1 celery stick, chopped

250ml (9fl oz) white wine

a small bunch of parsley

1 scant teaspoon salt

pepper

55g (2oz) butter, melted and mixed with 1 tablespoon chopped fresh parsley

triangular croûtons of bread fried in butter, to serve

SERVES 4–6 **Water souchy is the anglicised name for *waterzooi*, a Flemish dish. It made several appearances in eighteenth-century English cookery books as a method for freshwater fish, usually perch, simply boiled in water with a bunch of parsley. 'This seems a very insipid Dish in the Description, but there is something very pretty in the Taste of the small Fish this way,' wrote Martha Bradley in 1756. Later versions add wine and make a fish stock.**

1 Remove any skin or bones from the fish, put them in a pan and cut the flesh into neat serving pieces. Keep this cool.

2 Add the onion, carrot and celery to the fish skin and bones and cover with water. Bring to the boil and cook quickly for about 20 minutes to make a stock. Strain, discarding the debris.

3 Take a pan in which the fish pieces will fit in a single layer. Pour in the wine, bring to the boil and cook for a few minutes. Add the bunch of parsley and the pieces of fish and pour in the stock. It should just cover the fish – if it doesn't, add a little water. Season with salt and a little pepper and bring to the boil. Simmer until the fish is just cooked; this will take about 7–10 minutes, depending on the thickness of the pieces.

4 Remove from the heat and divide the fish between 4–6 soup bowls. Pour some of the cooking liquor over each portion. Pour the warm parsley butter into a small bowl and serve this and the fried bread croûtons separately.

Fish Pie

Ingredients

*800–900g (1¾–2lb) floury
potatoes, cut in chunks*

30g (1oz) butter

55ml (2fl oz) milk

*55g (2oz) coarsely grated Gruyère
or Cheddar cheese*

600g (1lb 5oz) cod or haddock fillet

250g (9oz) peeled prawns

Fish stock

skin and any bones from the fish

shells from the prawns

150ml (5fl oz) white wine

2 celery sticks, chopped

*1 leek, trimmed, washed and
cut in thick slices*

a few sprigs fresh parsley

1 small carrot, quartered

700ml (1¼ pints) water

Sauce

30g (1oz) butter

30g (1oz) plain flour

85g (3oz) crème fraîche

salt and pepper

SERVES 4

This fish pie is of the type common in British cookery during the twentieth century, with mashed potato on top; a comforting dish when it is well made. This version uses a sauce recipe derived from French cookery, which is particularly good.

1 Put all the ingredients for the stock into a saucepan, bring to the boil and then reduce the heat and simmer for 25–30 minutes. Strain, discarding the debris.

2 To make the sauce, melt the butter in a clean pan, stir in the flour and allow to cook for a moment without browning. Stir in about 300ml (½ pint) of the fish stock to make a smooth sauce. Allow to cook gently for 5–10 minutes, adding a little more stock if it seems on the thick side (the remainder of the stock can be frozen if you have no immediate use for it). Add the crème fraîche and season with salt and pepper to taste.

3 Meanwhile, boil the potatoes until tender, then drain well and mash with the butter, milk and cheese. Season to taste with some salt and pepper.

4 Cut the fish fillets into neat slices about 2cm (¾in) wide and arrange them in the bottom of a deep ovenproof dish. Scatter the peeled prawns over the top. Pour in the sauce and top with the mashed potato. Use a fork to roughen the surface.

5 Bake the fish pie in a preheated oven at 190°C, 375°F, Gas mark 5 for 30–40 minutes, until the top is crisp and golden.

Vegetables

Cornish Potato Cakes

Ingredients

2–3 floury potatoes, total weight 500g (1lb 2oz), boiled in the skins and allowed to cool (but they must not be chilled)

55g (2oz) shredded beef suet

55g (2oz) plain flour, plus extra for dusting

1 teaspoon baking powder

a generous pinch of salt

MAKES 18

Floury maincrop potatoes are essential for making these tasty little cakes.

1 Preheat the oven to 200°C, 400°F, Gas mark 6. Peel the boiled potatoes and then crumble them into small pieces. Mix with the shredded beef suet, flour, baking powder and salt to make a smooth, slightly sticky paste. Don't overwork it.

2 Roll the paste out on a well-floured board or work surface to a thickness of 1cm (½in). Cut into 18 squares and place them on a baking sheet.

3 Bake the potato cakes in the preheated oven for 10–15 minutes, until browned and crisp. Eat them immediately.

Bake the potato cakes until golden brown and crisp

Devonshire Stew

SERVES 4 **Recorded by Florence White back in the 1920s, this is not really a 'stew' at all but is more like the traditional bubble and squeak. It is an excellent accompaniment to ham, bacon or eggs.**

Ingredients

500g (1lb 2oz) medium potatoes, not too floury (Desirée work well)

2 medium onions

250g (9oz) cabbage, cut in 2–3 wedges

1 teaspoon salt

plenty of pepper

beef dripping or butter

1 Boil the potatoes, whole and unpeeled, until they are almost done. Peel the onions but leave whole, and boil them until tender. Boil the cabbage briefly and press it in a colander with a plate on top to squeeze out as much water as possible.

2 When the potatoes are cool enough to handle, peel them and cut into long narrow chip shapes. Shred the onion and cabbage. Mix everything together and season well.

3 Heat the dripping or butter in a large frying pan and add the vegetables, stirring until the mixture is nicely browned (you may need to do this in 2 batches). Serve very hot.

This is more like traditional bubble and squeak than a stew

Boulangère Potatoes

SERVES 4-6 | **Although this rustic dish has French origins, it was popularised in Britain during the love affair with French food in the mid-twentieth century. Marcel Boulestin gave an early version in his book *Simple French Cooking for English Homes* (1930). It is similar to *tiesen nionod*, a Welsh dish of onions and potatoes baked like a gratin (see page 170).**

1 Preheat the oven to 180–190°C, 350–375°F, Gas mark 4–5. Fry the onions gently in butter to soften them, but don't let them colour (they can be blanched in boiling water if you prefer). Slice the potatoes really thinly.

2 Grease a shallow ovenproof dish with butter and arrange the potatoes and onions in layers, seasoning well as you go. Finish with a neat layer of overlapping potato slices. Dot the top with butter and then pour in the stock – it should come almost to the top of the dish.

3 Bake in the preheated oven until the potatoes are soft and the surface nicely browned. A little extra (hot) stock or water can be added during cooking if the dish seems to be drying out, but this dish is better for not swimming in liquid.

Ingredients

2 large onions, thinly sliced

unsalted butter

about 750g (1lb 10oz) baking potatoes, peeled and thinly sliced

salt and pepper

150ml (5fl oz) well-flavoured stock

Summer Green Vegetable Stew

Ingredients

200g (7oz) asparagus

100g (3½oz) broad beans (after podding)

100g (3½oz) peas (after podding)

500g (1lb 2oz) other vegetables, such as French, runner or bobby beans; mangetouts or sugar peas; small courgettes; Florentine fennel; young, small globe artichokes

150ml (5fl oz) olive oil

1 large onion, finely chopped

a bouquet garni of 1 bay leaf, fresh thyme and parsley sprigs, plus summer savory if available

300ml (½ pint) white wine

1 teaspoon salt

pesto, to serve (optional)

Butterballs

60g (2¼oz) fresh white breadcrumbs

30g (1oz) butter

1 egg yolk

a pinch of salt

1 tablespoon chopped fresh herbs, to taste, such as parsley, chives, tarragon and chervil

SERVES 4

This recipe makes the most of late spring and summer vegetables. It is essentially an easy-going mixture of the best from the garden or the market. The onion, asparagus, broad beans and peas are essential; make up the remaining weight with a selection of the other vegetables listed.

1 Make sure all the vegetables are washed and prepared as appropriate. Discard any woody bits off the asparagus stems and cut the rest in 2cm (¾in) lengths. Trim the green beans and cut in 2cm (¾in) lengths. Trim the courgettes and cut in short lengths if very small, or dice 1–2cm (½ –¾in) square if larger.

2 Trim the fennel, discarding any tough or blemished outer layers, and cut into dice. Trim the stems and cut the tops off the globe artichokes, then scoop out and discard the thistle-like choke from the centre. Cut them in quarters.

3 Heat the oil in a large flameproof casserole. Add the onion and bouquet garni. Cook over a very low heat until the onions start to turn translucent. Then add the asparagus, broad beans, peas and whatever other vegetables have been chosen. Heat through, turning them all well in the oil. Add the wine and salt. Bring to a simmer and cook gently, turning occasionally, until all the vegetables are cooked through but not too soft. Taste and check the seasoning.

4 Make the butterballs by whizzing the breadcrumbs, butter, egg yolk and salt in a blender. Stir in the chopped herbs and form into about 20 little balls the size of hazelnuts. Drop them into the cooked vegetable mixture and simmer for 5 minutes.

5 Serve in deep bowls, adding pesto if you wish, and hand round some crusty bread or toast separately.

Champ

SERVES 4 **This is classic Irish comfort food. The standard version uses spring onions but you could try chives instead. Serve simply with boiled bacon, sliced off the piece, and some boiled cabbage.**

Ingredients

500–600g (1lb 2oz–1lb 5oz) potatoes, peeled and cut in chunks

salt and pepper

100ml (3½fl oz) buttermilk

a handful of chives or 6 spring onions

butter, to serve

1 Boil the potatoes until tender. Drain, season with salt and pepper and mash with a little of the buttermilk.

2 Chop the greenery into short lengths, add to the buttermilk and warm until almost boiling. Beat the mixture into the mashed potato. Serve very hot in individual portions, each one shaped into a mound with a hollow, adding butter to each.

Parsnip Fritters

SERVES 4 **Root vegetables, such as carrots, parsnips and beetroot, have long been a feature of the East Anglian landscape. This recipe is an adaptation of a nineteenth-century method for cooking parsnips.**

Ingredients

400g (14oz) parsnips, cut into chunks

30g (1oz) plain flour

salt and pepper

1 egg white

oil or fat, for deep-frying

1 Boil the parsnips until soft, then drain and mash. Stir in the flour. Season with a little salt and a generous grind of pepper. Beat the egg white to soft peak stage and stir into the mixture.

2 Heat the oil or fat in a deep fryer and drop teaspoons of the parsnip mixture into it. Cook for 3–4 minutes, until golden brown and slightly puffed. Drain on kitchen paper, sprinkle with salt and serve alongside grilled steak.

Roast Parsnips

SERVES 4-6 **This is a root vegetable that goes well with roast beef. Parsnips are considered to be at their best in winter, after the first frosts – freezing temperatures convert some of the starch in the living roots into sugar, and this caramelises when they are cooked. Always look for ones that are fresh and firm; flabby parsnips don't cook well.**

Ingredients

500g (1lb 2oz) parsnips

about 55g (2oz) fat for roasting, such as dripping from beef or pork or lard

salt

1 Wash and trim the parsnips and scrape off the skin with a peeler. Cut, on the diagonal, into slices about 5mm (¼in) thick. They can be parboiled for about 5 minutes, but if they are good and fresh, this isn't necessary. Put the fat in a roasting tin in a preheated hot oven at 220°C, 425°F, Gas mark 7.

2 Drain the parsnips well if parboiled, then tip into the hot fat (protect your hands with oven gloves). Turn them around in the fat, sprinkle with a little salt and roast for 10 minutes.

3 Turn the heat down to 190°C, 375°F, Gas mark 5 and cook for another 20–30 minutes, stirring occasionally so that they develop nicely browned surfaces. Drain well before serving.

Parsnips are at their best in winter after the first frosts

Root Vegetable Pie

Ingredients

300g (10½oz) Jerusalem artichokes

300g (10½oz) celeriac

300g (10½oz) leek (white part only)

300g (10½oz) waxy potatoes, such as Anya or Pink Fir Apple

115g (4oz) well-flavoured cheese, such as Cheddar or Blue Stilton, cut in thin slices or crumbled

40g (1½oz) butter

40g (1½oz) flour, plus extra for dusting

565ml (1 pint) milk

salt and pepper

a pinch of grated nutmeg

1 quantity puff pastry (see page 300)

beaten egg, cream or milk, to glaze

SERVES 4

The original of this recipe was Woolton Pie, which became infamous during World War II. It was a dish of root vegetables, such as swede and parsnip, cooked under an oatmeal pie crust – plain as plain could be – but we have updated it with some more unusual vegetables to create a delicious dish.

1 Wash the Jerusalem artichokes, put them in a pan, cover with water and simmer for 10–15 minutes, or until just tender. Drain and cover with cold water; once they are cool enough to handle, peel off the papery skin. Cut the flesh into julienne strips. Wash and peel the celeriac and cut into julienne strips. Wash the leek and slice into thin rings. Wash the potatoes, peel them if desired and cut into julienne strips.

2 Put the artichokes in a deep pie dish, scatter over about a quarter of the cheese, and repeat with the other vegetables and remaining cheese.

3 Melt the butter in a pan, stir in the flour, then add the milk to make a sauce, stirring with a wooden spoon until well thickened and smooth. Season with salt, pepper and a grating of nutmeg. Pour this over the vegetables in the dish.

4 Dust a work surface with the extra flour and roll out the pastry. Use it to cover the dish, trimming the edges and making decorative leaves. Make a hole in the centre for steam to escape and brush the pastry with egg, cream or milk.

5 Bake the pie in a preheated hot oven at 220°C, 425°F, Gas mark 7 for 20 minutes, then turn the heat down to 180°C, 350°F, Gas mark 4 and cook for a further 40 minutes.

Tiesen Nionod

SERVES 4

This Welsh dish is similar to a gratin, and tastes good if served with a roast of Welsh lamb.

Ingredients

85–100g (3–3½oz) butter, plus extra for greasing

900g (2lb) potatoes, preferably a waxy variety such as Desirée, peeled and thinly sliced

400g (14oz) onions, chopped

salt and pepper

1 Butter the inside of a baking dish or deep cake tin. Arrange a layer of potato slices over the bottom, then add a layer of onions, more potatoes, and so on until all the vegetables are used. Season the layers with salt and pepper, dot with butter and finish with potato. Cover with foil, pressing the vegetables down well.

2 Bake in a preheated oven at 180°C, 350°F, Gas mark 4 for 1–1½ hours, until golden brown and the potatoes are tender. A small joint of lamb can be cooked on top, in which case reduce the amount of butter to 25g (1oz) and add a little stock.

Roast Potatoes

SERVES 4-6

Roast potatoes are the defining element of 'a proper roast'. King Edward, a potato variety with almost iconic status in Britain, probably has the best flavour, and can develop a fantastic crisp crust and melting interior. Wilja and Desirée are also good; Cara and Romano should produce reasonable results.

Ingredients

500g (1lb 2oz) potatoes, peeled and cut into large chunks

30g (1oz) goose fat or beef dripping

salt

1 Preheat the oven to 200–220°C, 400–425°F, Gas mark 6–7. Put the potatoes in a pan, just cover with cold water and bring to the boil. Boil for 5–7 minutes, then drain well.

2 Put the fat in a roasting tin and place in the oven until very hot. Take it out and add the potatoes. Turn them over in the hot fat, sprinkle with salt and roast for 40–50 minutes. Turn once or twice during cooking, and add a little more salt each time.

Souffléed Green Pea Pancakes

Ingredients

200g (7oz) green peas, fresh or frozen

a pinch of salt

about 15g (½oz) butter

2–3 tablespoons finely grated Parmesan cheese

2 eggs, separated

a little sunflower or vegetable oil, for frying

Crowdie sauce

about 140g (5oz) crowdie or other soft, creamy cheese

1–2 tablespoons milk

1 tablespoon finely chopped mint

a little grated lemon zest and juice

SERVES 3-4 **The Scots have taken to fresh green peas with enthusiasm, as a vegetable or added to broths. The idea of a soufflé based on fresh peas occurs as an *haute cuisine* version in *The Cookery Book of Lady Clark of Tillypronie* (1909), as well as a more homely recipe in the *Scottish Women's Rural Institutes Cookery Book* (1952). We have taken the idea further.**

1 The crowdie sauce is better made a little in advance to allow the flavours to develop. Mix all the ingredients together to give a smooth sauce, tasting until you feel that a pleasant balance of flavours has been achieved. Chill until needed.

2 To make the pancakes, put the peas in a pan, add a pinch of salt and a little boiling water – no more than halfway up to the top of the peas. Bring to the boil over a high heat, then turn the heat down and cook, uncovered, until the peas are tender and almost all the water has evaporated – don't boil dry.

3 When the peas are cooked, tip them into a blender and purée. Tip into a bowl and stir in the butter and Parmesan. Let it cool for 10 minutes, then add the egg yolks. Whisk the egg whites to the soft peak stage and fold into the pea mixture.

4 Heat a large heavy frying pan and add a little oil – just enough to grease the bottom. Drop generous tablespoons of the mixture into the pan (you will have to cook the pancakes in batches) and fry gently. The bases of the little cakes will brown gently and set. Run a spatula underneath to flip them over and cook lightly on the other side. Keep them warm until all the pancakes are cooked, then serve immediately with the sauce.

Peas with Cream

SERVES 4 **The idea of eating fresh green peas became fashionable during the seventeenth century. They were often cooked with butter and herbs in the manner we still know as *à la française*, but there were variations, such as adding cream. Serve with bread for a light lunch or supper, or to accompany egg or cheese dishes, or plainly grilled meat or fish.**

Ingredients

2–4 lettuce hearts, depending on size; use Little Gem or Cos

20g (¾oz) butter

250g (9oz) green peas (shelled weight)

2 tablespoons water

½ teaspoon salt

½ teaspoon sugar

a pinch of grated nutmeg

1 teaspoon butter kneaded with 1 teaspoon flour (optional)

4 tablespoons double cream

a mixture of fresh chives, mint, chervil or tarragon – enough to make about 2 tablespoons when finely chopped

1 Remove any raggedy outer leaves from the lettuces. Cut in half lengthways, wash them and shake as dry as possible.

2 Place a frying pan over a very gentle heat and melt the butter in it. Add the lettuces, cut-side down. Put the peas in around them. Add the water, remembering that the lettuces will produce more liquid as they cook. Sprinkle in the salt and sugar and then grate in a little nutmeg.

3 Cover the pan closely (use foil if it doesn't have a lid) and cook, very gently, for 25 minutes. Check every few minutes at the start to make sure that it isn't drying up, and towards the end to see how much juice the vegetables have yielded. If there seems to be more than a couple of tablespoonfuls, remove the cover for the last few minutes.

4 At the end of the cooking time, remove the lettuces to a warmed serving dish (if there still seems to be a lot of juice in the pan with the peas, distribute the flour and butter mixture over the surface and heat gently, shaking the pan until the sauce thickens). Add the cream, stir well and heat until nearly boiling, then pour over the lettuce. Sprinkle with the herbs and serve.

Stewed Red Cabbage

Ingredients

1 small red cabbage

100g (3½oz) ham in one piece

20g (¾oz) butter

1–2 tablespoons muscovado sugar

70ml (2½fl oz) malt vinegar

200ml (7fl oz) meat stock

salt, pepper and allspice

SERVES 4-6 **Red cabbage is a good accompaniment to roast pork or sausages. This delicious version is based on a nineteenth-century recipe from Suffolk.**

1 Cut the cabbage in quarters, remove the stem and slice the leaves thinly. Put the ham and butter in a casserole, and put the cabbage on top. Add the sugar, vinegar and stock.

2 Cook in a preheated cool oven at 140°C, 275°F, Gas mark 1 for 2½ hours. Watch it doesn't dry out. Taste and adjust the seasoning, adding salt and a little more sugar if desired. Grind a little pepper and allspice over just before serving.

Mushrooms in Cream

Ingredients

6–8 button mushrooms

salt and pepper

1 tablespoon chopped fresh parsley

1–2 sprigs fresh thyme, chopped

1 small garlic clove, crushed

85ml (3fl oz) single cream

SERVES 1 **The Derbyshire childhood of the children's author Alison Uttley is beautifully evoked in her book *Recipes From an Old Farmhouse*, in which she describes cooking mushrooms in saucers of cream for breakfast or tea. Juicy, delicately flavoured field mushrooms are best if you can get hold of them.**

1 Wipe the mushrooms and trim the stems close to the caps. Place, cap down, in a small shallow ovenproof dish. Sprinkle with salt and pepper, the herbs and garlic. Pour the cream over.

2 Bake, uncovered, in a preheated hot oven at 220°C, 425°F, Gas mark 7 for 20 minutes, or until the mushrooms are cooked. Baste with the cream halfway through cooking. Serve on toast, or leave in the dish and mop up the juices with bread.

Braised Celery

SERVES 4 **This has been in the English cookery repertoire for at least 200 years. It is a good side dish for roasts of game, especially venison, or as a separate vegetable course with some crusty bread.**

Ingredients

2 large heads celery

15g (½oz) butter

1 medium onion, finely chopped

1 small carrot, finely chopped

1 small slice of turnip, finely chopped

a bouquet garni of 1 bay leaf and some fresh thyme and parsley sprigs

500ml (18fl oz) strong beef stock

salt

croûtons fried in butter, to garnish

1 Trim the heads of celery, removing any stringy outer stems. Cut in half lengthways, wash well and blanch in boiling water. Cut in half crossways as well if the stems are very long.

2 Melt the butter in a pan that will hold the celery neatly in one layer. Add the onion, carrot and turnip and cover. Sweat gently for 15 minutes, then add the celery, cut-side down. Add the bouquet garni and pour in two-thirds of the stock. Simmer gently for 2 hours. Add more stock as it evaporates, but towards the end of cooking let it reduce to a fairly concentrated glaze.

3 Remove the celery and put it on a warmed serving dish. Taste the cooking liquid and add seasoning if required. Strain it over the celery and garnish generously with the croûtons.

Puréed Sprouts

SERVES 4 **Brussels sprouts are delicious puréed, and this vegetable side dish is good with game birds.**

Ingredients

salt and pepper

500g (1lb 2oz) Brussels sprouts, trimmed

120ml (4fl oz) single cream

1 Bring a saucepan of lightly salted water to the boil. Add the sprouts and cook until just tender. Drain well in a colander.

2 Put them in a food processor with the cream and seasoning to taste. Don't overdo the processing – you should be left with a beautiful pale green purée, which is lightly flecked with darker green, like a piece of jade.

Onions with a Cream Sauce and Wensleydale Cheese

SERVES 4 **An onion could provide a complete meal for a countryman or woman – a boiled or baked onion used to be especially popular, as in this recipe, which uses Yorkshire's best-known cheese.**

1 Peel the onions but leave them whole. Simmer them gently in a saucepan of water until they are tender (the timing depends on their size, but test after 30 minutes).

2 To make the sauce, melt the butter and add the flour to make a roux. Gradually blend in the milk and stir constantly until the sauce thickens. Allow it to cook gently on the lowest possible heat for 10–15 minutes. Add the cream, taste and add the seasonings.

3 Split each onion in half and arrange in a shallow ovenproof dish. Pour the white sauce over, scatter the cheese on top and flash under a preheated hot grill to melt the cheese.

Ingredients

4 large, mild onions

30g (1oz) butter

2 tablespoons plain flour

250ml (9fl oz) milk

85ml (3fl oz) double cream

salt, pepper and a little grated nutmeg

55g (2oz) Wensleydale cheese, grated

An onion could once provide a complete meal

Ragoo of Onions and Mushrooms

Ingredients

2 tablespoons olive oil

1 small onion, very finely chopped

1 celery stick, very finely chopped

1 medium carrot, very finely chopped

115g (4oz) lean unsmoked bacon or gammon, very finely chopped

400ml (14fl oz) well-flavoured stock

a bouquet garni of fresh parsley, thyme and marjoram sprigs (optional)

400g (14oz) shallots or very small onions, peeled

200g (7oz) button mushrooms, trimmed

salt and pepper

SERVES 4

'Ragoo' was the eighteenth-century English cook's phonetic rendition of the French *ragoût*. Complex mixtures requiring two or three different meaty stocks, these dishes were all the rage. They were used as sauces and garnishes, or as dishes in their own right. This one is very good with chicken but can also be served with beef, mutton or game. A good meaty stock based on chicken or veal, plus some ham, bacon or gammon, is essential.

1 Heat the oil in a saucepan. Add the onion, celery and carrot and fry briskly, stirring frequently until the vegetables begin to caramelise and turn golden brown at the edges. Add the bacon or gammon and continue frying for another 5–10 minutes. Any trimmings from the mushrooms can be added, too. Pour in the stock, and then add the bouquet garni, if using. When the mixture comes to the boil, turn it down to the lowest possible simmer and leave to cook until reduced by about half.

2 Put the shallots and mushrooms in a clean pan. Strain the reduced stock over them, pressing so that all the flavoursome juices pass through (but don't rub any of the solids through). Continue to cook very gently, stirring from time to time. By the time the onions are tender (about 45 minutes), the stock should be reduced to a few spoonfuls of thick, slightly syrupy liquid, just coating the vegetables. Taste and adjust the seasoning.

This is very good served with chicken

Baking and Teatime

Light Sponge Cake

Ingredients

55g (2oz) butter, plus extra for greasing

200g (7oz) granulated or caster sugar

2 large or 3 medium eggs

140g (5oz) self-raising flour, sifted

a pinch of salt

1 teaspoon baking powder

120ml (4fl oz) milk

2–3 drops vanilla essence

150ml (¼ pint) double cream, whipped

200g (7oz) strawberries, raspberries or other berries

icing sugar, for dusting

SERVES 8 **This is a recipe from Chirk Castle in Wales where afternoon tea was always a very elegant but small meal consisting of some sandwiches the size of a postage stamp. Sometimes, in cold weather, a dish of hot buttered muffins or warm scones was also served. This cake is quick and easy to make, and is especially delicious served with some fresh fruit and whipped cream. It is ideal for freezing.**

1 Preheat the oven to 170°C, 325°F, Gas mark 3. Lightly grease and line a 20cm (8in) round cake tin.

2 Beat together the sugar and eggs until thick and creamy. Add the flour, salt and baking powder and mix well. Put the milk in a small pan and heat gently. Melt the butter in the milk and bring to the boil. When boiling, add to the flour mixture with the vanilla essence and beat well to give a runny consistency. Spoon the mixture into the prepared tin and bang it sharply on the table to remove any air bubbles.

3 Bake the cake in the preheated oven for 20–25 minutes, until a skewer comes out clean. Remove from the oven and let the cake cool in the tin for 15 minutes before turning it out on to a wire rack to cool completely.

4 Cut the cake in half horizontally and cover one sponge with whipped cream and strawberries or raspberries (or a mixture of both). Place the other sponge on top, then dust lightly with some icing sugar and serve cut into slices.

Caraway Cake or Seed Cake

Ingredients

170g (6oz) butter, plus extra for greasing

170g (6oz) caster sugar

3 eggs

3 teaspoons caraway seeds

225g (8oz) plain flour

a pinch of salt

1 teaspoon baking powder

1 tablespoon ground almonds

1 tablespoon milk

SERVES 8-10

Caraway cake was the original seed cake, and it was very popular in the early nineteenth century, when the seeds would have been comfits – seeds dipped in sugar. This is in the English tradition of plain cakes – perfect at coffee time when you want something that is not too rich.

1 Preheat the oven to 170°C, 325°F, Gas mark 3. Grease and line a 23cm (9in) round cake tin.

2 Cream together the butter and sugar until fluffy and pale. Add the eggs, one at a time, beating well between each addition, and then mix in the caraway seeds. Sift the flour, salt and baking powder together and fold gently into the mixture. Then add the ground almonds and milk. Spoon the mixture into the prepared tin and level the top.

3 Bake in the preheated oven for approximately 1 hour, or until the cake is well risen and firm to the touch. Allow to cool in the tin before turning out the cake. Serve cut into slices.

Hazelnut Cake

Ingredients

melted butter, for greasing

170g (6oz) caster sugar, plus extra for dusting

3 large eggs, separated

juice of ½ lemon

55g (2oz) hazelnuts, skins on, finely ground

30g (1oz) plain flour, sifted

120ml (4fl oz) whipping cream, whipped to soft peaks

115g (4oz) fresh raspberries

SERVES 8

The crunchy texture of the hazelnuts contrasts pleasingly with the raspberries in this light sponge, which is filled with whipped cream.

1 Preheat the oven to 180°C, 350°F, Gas mark 4. Brush the inside of a 20cm (8in) round cake tin with melted butter and dust lightly with caster sugar.

2 Whisk the egg yolks and sugar together until thick and pale. Add the lemon juice. Gently fold in the ground hazelnuts, then the flour in a figure-of-eight movement with a metal spoon.

3 Whisk the egg whites until they hold a stiff peak. Stir a third of the egg whites into the hazelnut mixture to slacken it off, then gently fold in the remaining whites. Pour the mixture into the prepared cake tin.

4 Bake in the preheated oven for 35–40 minutes, until firm to the touch. Cool in the tin before turning out the cake. Carefully slice the cake in half horizontally and fill it with the whipped cream and raspberries.

This light sponge is filled with cream and raspberries

Saffron Cake

SERVES 8-10 **This is not a cake in the modern sense, but a traditional Cornish fruit bread, which is lightly spiced with saffron and served sliced and buttered.**

1 Put the saffron in a bowl, pour the boiling water over it and leave to infuse overnight. Mix 100g (3½oz) of the flour, a pinch of sugar, the yeast and the tepid water, and leave it for about 30 minutes, until frothy.

2 Rub the fat into the remaining flour. Add the salt, remaining sugar and beaten egg, the yeast mixture and the saffron water. Mix to a coherent dough, adding a little more tepid water if necessary. Knead well, cover the bowl with clingfilm and leave to rise in a warm place for about 1 hour.

3 Knock back and knead in the fruit and peel. Place in a greased 1.2 litre (2 pint) loaf tin and prove (leave in a warm place to rise again) for about 1 hour.

4 Bake in a preheated oven at 220°C, 425°F, Gas mark 7 for 40 minutes, or until the loaf sounds hollow when you tap it on the base with your knuckles. Turn out and cool on a wire rack. Eat thinly sliced, spread with butter.

Ingredients

a generous pinch of saffron threads

3 tablespoons boiling water

500g (1lb 2oz) strong plain white flour

100g (3½oz) caster sugar

1 tablespoon dried yeast

100ml (3½fl oz) tepid water

100g (3½oz) lard or butter, plus extra for greasing

1 teaspoon salt

1 egg, beaten

250g (9oz) currants

30g (1oz) candied peel, chopped

Serve this fruit bread sliced and buttered

Carrot Cake with Lime Topping

Ingredients

butter, for greasing

2 eggs

100g (3½oz) light soft brown sugar

85ml (3fl oz) sunflower, vegetable or corn oil

100g (3½oz) self-raising flour, sifted

170g (6oz) grated carrot

1 teaspoon ground cinnamon

55g (2oz) shredded coconut

Lime topping

85g (3oz) cream cheese

85g (3oz) butter, softened

55g (2oz) icing sugar

grated zest of 1 lime

toasted coconut and grated lime zest, to decorate (optional)

SERVES 8

This indulgent cake should be eaten with little pastry forks. These small, three-pronged forks developed from Victorian dessert forks in the second half of the nineteenth century. In order to exert a little pressure on a fruit tartlet or slice of cake, the first two narrow prongs of the fork were fused to make a wider one that acted as a cutting edge.

1 Preheat the oven to 190°C, 375°F, Gas mark 5. Grease and line a 900g (2lb) loaf tin or a 18cm (7in) round cake tin.

2 Beat together the eggs and sugar until very creamy. Add the oil and beat hard. Fold in the flour, grated carrot, cinnamon and coconut, and turn the mixture into the prepared tin. Smooth the top, then slightly hollow out the middle.

3 Bake in the preheated oven for 35–40 minutes, until golden and well risen and a skewer comes out clean. Remove from the oven and turn out on to a wire rack to cool.

4 To make the topping, beat the cream cheese, butter, icing sugar and lime zest together until light and creamy, then spread over the top of the cake. Make a pattern with the prongs of a fork and sprinkle with toasted coconut and grated lime zest.

Shrewsbury Cakes

MAKES 40 **Recipes for these little cakes, which are named after Shrewsbury in the heart of the Welsh Marches, have changed over the years from thick, delicately spiced shortcakes to biscuits with currants in them. This version is based on an old recipe in a manuscript of 1847, with the addition of flavours that recall eighteenth-century recipes.**

Ingredients

250g (9oz) caster sugar

250g (9oz) butter, softened

370g (13oz) plain flour, plus extra for dusting

½ teaspoon ground cinnamon

½ teaspoon grated nutmeg

1 egg yolk

1 tablespoon sherry

1 tablespoon rosewater (or use extra sherry)

¼ teaspoon salt

caraway seeds (optional)

1 Mix the sugar and butter, stirring until well amalgamated and soft. Add the flour and ground spices, the egg yolk, sherry and rosewater. Mix thoroughly and add the salt and caraway seeds, if using. A little extra sherry or rosewater may be needed, but try not to let the dough become sticky. Allow the mixture to rest for 30 minutes.

2 Roll out on a floured surface to 5mm (¼in) thick and cut out into thin rounds – you should get about 40. Place them on baking trays and bake in a preheated oven at 170°C, 325°F, Gas mark 3 for about 15 minutes. Take care not to let them brown.

3 Transfer the biscuits to a wire rack – they will crisp up as they cool. Store in an airtight container.

These currant biscuits are delicately spiced

Maids of Honour

MAKES 14 **Tradition says that these little sweet cheese tarts are named after the ladies-in-waiting to Queen Caroline, wife of George II, who reigned from 1727 to 1760. She lived in a palace in Richmond, Surrey, where, on Richmond Green, a terrace of lovely houses still stands called Maids of Honour Row. Newens, the last of the famous Kew tea rooms, still sells Maids of Honour, made to a secret recipe.**

1 The day before you want to bake the Maids of Honour, heat the milk to blood temperature, stir in a pinch of salt and add rennet, as directed on the bottle. When the curd has set and cooled, transfer it to a clean square of muslin or a jelly bag and allow the whey to drip out overnight.

2 The following day, rub the curd through a sieve with the butter. Beat in the egg yolks and brandy, then stir in the almonds, sugar, cinnamon, lemon juice and zest.

3 Roll out the puff pastry very thinly on a lightly floured surface and cut into 14 rounds with a plain cutter. Using a fork, prick the centres of the rounds lightly a few times – otherwise your maids may go head-over-heels in the oven. Line the patty tins with the rounds and put a generous teaspoon of the curd mixture in each. Scatter a few currants on top of each one.

4 Bake the pastry rounds in a preheated hot oven at 220°C, 425°F, Gas mark 7 for 7 minutes, until the pastry is risen and nicely browned. Cool on a wire rack.

Ingredients

500ml (18fl oz) whole milk

a pinch of salt

rennet

100g (3½oz) butter at room temperature

2 egg yolks

2 teaspoons brandy

12 almonds, blanched and chopped

30g (1oz) caster sugar

1 teaspoon ground cinnamon

juice and grated zest of ½ lemon

250g (9oz) puff pastry (see page 300)

plain flour, for dusting

4 tablespoons currants

Grasmere Gingerbread

SERVES 16 **The authentic Grasmere gingerbread is sold from a little shop in this pretty Lake District village. It is absolutely delicious and the shop recipe is a secret. This version comes from Marion Hayton.**

Ingredients

225g (8oz) butter, plus extra for greasing

450g (1lb) plain flour

225g (8oz) light brown sugar

1 teaspoon bicarbonate of soda

1 teaspoon cream of tartar

2 teaspoons ground ginger

a pinch of salt

1 tablespoon golden syrup

granulated sugar, for sprinkling

1 In a large bowl, rub the butter into the flour. Add the other dry ingredients and mix well. Add the golden syrup and rub into the mixture until it is crumbly.

2 Grease a baking sheet and press the mixture on to it in a block 1cm (½in) thick. Don't be alarmed if it's crumbly.

3 Bake the gingerbread in a preheated oven at 150°C, 300°F, Gas mark 2 until golden brown. While it's still hot, sprinkle with a little granulated sugar. Allow to cool for 15 minutes and then cut into fingers.

Serve this gingerbread cut into fingers

Mrs Watson's Iced Ginger Shortcake

Ingredients

200g (7oz) butter

100g (3½oz) caster sugar

250g (9oz) flour (half plain and half self-raising)

1½ teaspoons ground ginger

Icing

70g (2½oz) butter

1 tablespoon golden syrup

1 teaspoon ground ginger

55g (2oz) icing sugar

SERVES 16

Mrs Watson's family farm is in Northumberland, where the green hills start to rise towards the Cheviots. These iced ginger shortcake fingers are really delicious and will keep well for several days.

1 Cream the butter with the caster sugar in a bowl. Mix the flour with the ginger and work into the creamed mixture.

2 Press the mixture into a shallow 22cm (8½in) square shallow cake tin and then bake in a preheated oven at 150–170°C, 300–325°F, Gas mark 2–3 for 40 minutes, until golden brown.

3 While the shortcake is still warm, make the icing. Melt the butter and syrup together. Add the ginger and icing sugar and stir thoroughly to give a smooth mixture with no white patches of icing sugar. Pour over the shortcake. Cut into fingers while still warm, then leave to cool in the tin.

Oatmeal Parkin

SERVES 12 **Parkin is a north-country name for gingerbread. There are probably as many recipes for parkin as there are cooks who bake it. It comes in several types – cake-like, biscuit-like or made with oatmeal. This 1930s' recipe from the Knaresborough area of Yorkshire is unusual since it is based on oatmeal (most recipes require some flour) and includes rum.**

1 Take an old-fashioned 24cm (9½in) square Yorkshire pudding tin, 5cm (2in) deep, or similar. Grease it well with some lard or butter. Preheat the oven to 150°C, 300°F, Gas mark 2.

2 Mix the oatmeal. salt, bicarbonate of soda and ground ginger together in a large bowl. Warm the golden syrup with the lard and butter until the fats have melted, then stir in the rum and cream. Pour on to the oatmeal mixture and stir well. Drop the parkin mix into the prepared tin.

3 Bake in the preheated oven for around 1½ hours, until the mixture feels set in the middle and is just starting to pull away from the edges of the tin. Cool in the tin, and then cut it. Keep it covered, not airtight, for a couple of days before eating.

Ingredients

30g (1oz) lard, plus extra for greasing

500g (1lb 2oz) medium oatmeal

¼ teaspoon salt

½ teaspoon bicarbonate of soda

2 teaspoons ground ginger

500g (1lb 2oz) golden syrup

30g (1oz) butter

3 tablespoons rum

1 tablespoon single cream

Parkin is a north-country name for gingerbread

Strawberry Shortcake

SERVES 6

Hampshire strawberries used to be famous, partly because they were the first to reach the London markets in the days before imported ones became commonplace. Only use the freshest, ripest strawberries when filling this delicious cake.

Ingredients

170g (6oz) butter, plus extra for greasing

170g (6oz) plain flour, plus extra for dusting

170g (6oz) caster sugar

a pinch of salt

1 egg, beaten

750g (1lb 10oz) strawberries

100ml (3½fl oz) whipping cream

1 Lightly grease 2 large baking sheets or trays. Mix the flour, sugar and salt. Rub in the butter, then stir in the beaten egg to make a soft, slightly sticky dough. Flour a work surface well, divide the dough in half and pat each one into a circle on the greased baking trays. Chill for 1 hour.

2 Preheat the oven to 170°C, 325°F, Gas mark 3. Bake the shortcakes in the preheated oven for 30–35 minutes, until lightly browned; if the mixture spreads a lot, neaten it by trimming it with a sharp knife while still hot. Cool on wire racks.

3 About 2 hours before eating, place one shortcake on a plate and cover it with strawberries – cut any that are very large in half. Place the other shortcake on top. Reserve a few of the best strawberries for decoration.

4 Just before serving, whip the cream until it holds its shape and spread over the top of the shortcake. Decorate with the reserved strawberries and serve.

Use only the freshest, ripest strawberries

Apple Cake

SERVES 8

Apple cakes frequently feature in books of Dorset and Somerset recipes. They are usually eaten warm, spread with butter, or served with custard or thick cream. This delicious version has been re-worked to emphasise the presence of the apples. Always use well-flavoured dessert apples.

Ingredients

140g (5oz) butter

140g (5oz) granulated sugar

2 eggs

300g (10½oz) self-raising flour

½ teaspoon salt

1 teaspoon ground cinnamon

100ml (3½fl oz) milk

400–450g (14oz–1lb) desert apples, peeled, cored and finely grated

1 tablespoon brandy or apple brandy

1 tablespoon caster sugar, ideally vanilla-flavoured

1 Cream the butter and sugar together until light and fluffy. Beat in the eggs. Sift the flour, salt and cinnamon together and add this to the creamed mixture. Add a little milk to slacken off, but don't overdo it; the mixture should be on the stiff side.

2 Put half the cake mixture into a 20cm (8in) cake tin, lined with non-stick baking parchment. Level it off, then make a hollow in the middle with the back of a spoon. Mix the grated apple with the brandy and put the mixture in the hollow. Don't let it touch the edges of the tin. Dollop the rest of the mixture over the top and smooth off, sealing the apple in the middle. Sprinkle with caster sugar.

3 Bake the cake in a preheated moderate oven at 190°C, 375°F, Gas mark 5 for 1 hour 10 minutes. Cool on a wire rack, then serve warm with some thick cream. The cake may be slightly puddingy in the middle, but it should still taste good.

Staffordshire Fruitcake

SERVES 10

This is one of the many variations of fruit cake that are found across Britain. The addition of ground almonds helps to keep it moist. It tastes even better if you can resist eating it straightaway and leave it to mature for a couple of weeks before cutting.

Ingredients

140g (5oz) butter, plus extra for greasing

450g (1lb) currants

225g (8oz) mixed candied peel, chopped

115g (4oz) ground almonds

225g (8oz) plain flour

140g (5oz) caster sugar

4 eggs

1 tablespoon black treacle

70ml (2½fl oz) brandy

1 teaspoon ground mace

grated zest of 1 lemon

1 teaspoon baking powder

1–2 tablespoons milk

1 Grease a 22cm (8½in) round cake tin and then line it with greaseproof paper or baking parchment. Preheat the oven to 170°C, 325°F, Gas mark 3.

2 Mix the currants, peel, ground almonds and 2 tablespoons of the flour together and set aside. Beat the butter and sugar together until light and pale. Beat in the eggs, one by one, alternating each with a tablespoon of flour. When all the flour has been added, warm the treacle and stir in with the brandy, mace, lemon zest and baking powder. Add a little milk if the mixture seems very dry. Finally, stir in the fruit mixture.

3 Spoon the mixture into the prepared tin and level the top. Bake in the preheated oven for 2½ hours. It is ready when a skewer comes out clean. Leave to cool, then wrap in foil and store in a cake tin.

Pitcaithly Bannock

SERVES 12 **This is a type of Scottish shortbread, which includes almonds and candied peel. Shortbread was an expression of the best of country produce – butter combined with fine white flour and sugar, which were expensive and desirable luxuries. The quality of the butter is of great importance, so look for really good butter made from cream from whole milk. You may be lucky and find farm-made butter; otherwise, that made with the milk of Ayrshire, Guernsey or Jersey cattle is a good choice.**

Ingredients

170g (6oz) plain flour

30g (1oz) rice flour, but if you can't get this, use an extra 30g (1oz) plain flour

30g (1oz) ground almonds

30g (1oz) candied citron or orange peel

115g (4oz) butter

85g (3oz) caster sugar

1 Dry the flour in a low oven (don't let it brown). Cool and sieve. Mix in the rice flour and ground almonds. Chop the candied peel very finely and add this to the flour.

2 Blend the butter and sugar until well mixed (traditionally this was done by rubbing them together on a board, but this is a potentially messy process, so it's better done in a bowl unless you are used to the method). Work in the dry ingredients. Don't knead the mixture, but press it together into a ball.

3 Put this on a sheet of baking parchment on a baking tray. Press out to a circle about 20cm (8in) in diameter. Pinch the edges to make a decorative border.

4 Bake in a preheated moderate oven at 170°C, 325°F, Gas mark 3 for about 30 minutes, or until golden. Allow to cool on the tray until firm, then transfer to a wire rack.

This is a type of Scottish shortbread

Walsingham Honey Cake

Ingredients

225g (8oz) butter, softened, plus extra for greasing

225g (8oz) light soft brown sugar

2 eggs, beaten

450g (1lb) plain flour, sifted

1 teaspoon ground ginger

1 teaspoon bicarbonate of soda

115g (4oz) raisins

55g (2oz) mixed candied peel

55g (2oz) glacé cherries, halved

300ml (½ pint) milk

85g (3oz) clear honey

85g (3oz) black treacle

Topping

3–4 tablespoons clear honey

40g (1½oz) light soft brown sugar

55g (2oz) butter

55g (2oz) flaked almonds

SERVES 9 **Little Walsingham in north Norfolk became an important place of pilgrimage when visions of the Virgin Mary were seen. The area also is famous for its bees and honey. For centuries, honey has been used to treat wounds; it has antibacterial properties and therefore helps the body to heal.**

1 Preheat the oven to 170°C, 325°F, Gas mark 3. Grease and line a 18cm (7in) square cake tin.

2 Beat together the butter and sugar until light and fluffy. Add the beaten eggs and beat again. Add the flour, ginger and bicarbonate of soda and beat well. Stir in the dried fruit, candied peel and cherries. Warm together the milk, honey and treacle and add gradually, beating well and making sure that all the ingredients are evenly distributed.

3 Turn the cake mixture into the prepared tin and bake in the preheated oven for 2 hours, until a skewer comes out clean. Remove from the oven and leave in the tin.

4 Make the topping: warm together the honey, sugar and butter and pour over the warm cake. Sprinkle with the flaked almonds and allow to cool completely in the tin before serving.

Sprinkle with flaked almonds before serving

Cornish Splits

MAKES 8

This is a delightful Cornish version of little breads, as recorded by Florence White in the 1930s. These rolls are delicious served split with home-made fruit jam and thick clotted cream.

Ingredients

1 tablespoon dried yeast

1 teaspoon granulated sugar

55ml (2fl oz) hand-hot milk

115g (4oz) butter, plus extra for greasing

30g (1oz) lard

750g (1lb 10oz) strong plain flour

1 teaspoon salt

400ml (14fl oz) tepid water

1 Cream the yeast with the sugar in the warm milk. Gently melt the butter and lard and add to the flour, together with the yeast mixture. Sprinkle in the salt. Add enough of the tepid water to make a dough.

2 Knead the dough for about 10 minutes, then cover and put in a warm place to rise. When it has doubled in size, knock it back and knead again. Divide it into 55g (2oz) pieces and shape into rolls. Place the rolls on a greased baking tray and leave them to prove in a warm place until doubled in size.

3 Bake in a preheated oven at 220°C, 425°F, Gas mark 7 for 20 minutes. On removing the rolls from the oven, rub them over with a butter paper and then wrap in a cloth to cool.

Serve split with jam and thick clotted cream

Cream Scones

MAKES 12 **This 'north country' recipe for the teatime classic was originally given by Florence White. Serve them warm, split in half and thickly buttered or with fruit jam and whipped or clotted cream.**

Ingredients

55g (2oz) butter, plus extra for greasing

500g (1lb 2oz) self-raising flour, plus extra for dusting

1 teaspoon salt

1 teaspoon cream of tartar

½ teaspoon bicarbonate of soda

2 eggs

150ml (¼ pint) double cream

about 200ml (7fl oz) milk

1 Preheat the oven to 220°C, 425°F, Gas mark 7. Lightly grease a large baking sheet.

2 In a large bowl, rub the butter into the flour. Stir in the salt and the raising agents. Beat the eggs and cream together and stir in well. Add enough milk to make a soft but not sticky dough and knead lightly.

3 Roll out the dough on a lightly floured board or work surface to approximately 2cm (¾in) thick and cut into 12 rounds with a plain or fluted cutter.

4 Put the scones on the prepared baking sheet and bake in the preheated oven for about 15 minutes, until well risen and golden brown. Allow to cool a little before serving.

Bake until well risen and golden brown

Singin' Hinnie

MAKES 2 | **This cake hails from the Northumbrian tradition of girdle baking. If you don't have a girdle (an iron baking sheet) you can use a heavy frying pan.**

Ingredients

400g (14oz) plain flour, plus extra for dusting

a generous pinch of salt

1 teaspoon baking powder

100g (3½oz) lard, plus extra for greasing

100g (3½oz) butter

140g (5oz) currants

2–3 tablespoons milk

butter, brown sugar and grated nutmeg, to serve

1 Mix the flour, salt and baking powder together in a large bowl. Rub in the lard and butter with your fingertips, and then stir in the currants and mix to a dough using the milk.

2 Divide the mixture in two and roll out on a lightly floured board to rounds, about 4cm (1½in) thick.

3 Heat a girdle or a large heavy frying pan, grease lightly with lard and place over a moderate heat. When it's hot, put a round on to cook, keeping an eye on the heat. It may take up to 15 minutes to bake. When the underside is brown, turn it over and cook the other side. Repeat with the other round.

4 Split the hinnies crossways, butter them well, sprinkle with brown sugar and nutmeg and eat warm.

Serve the buttered hinnies with brown sugar and nutmeg

210

Cumberland Girdle Cakes

SERVES 6-8 **These cakes also belong to the north-country method of baking on a flat iron plate called a girdle, which was suspended over the fire.**

1 Mix the flour, salt and baking powder together in a large bowl. Rub in the butter with your fingertips. Mix to a firm but not too sticky dough with the milk or cream.

2 Flour a work surface lightly and roll out the dough to a circle, about 5mm (¼in) thick.

3 Heat an iron girdle or large heavy frying pan and grease it lightly with butter. Put the cake on it and cook gently for 10–15 minutes. When it is golden brown underneath, turn it over and cook for another 5–10 minutes on the other side, or until it is golden. Cut into squares while still warm, then split and serve buttered on a hot dish.

Ingredients

85g (3oz) plain flour, plus extra for dusting

a pinch of salt

a generous pinch of baking powder

30g (1oz) butter, plus extra for greasing

70ml (2½fl oz) milk or single cream

These cakes were traditionally baked on an iron girdle

Fruit Loaf

Ingredients

300ml (½ pint) strong tea

450g (1lb) mixed dried fruit, such as sultanas, raisins and currants

butter, for greasing

170g (6oz) soft light brown sugar

340g (12oz) self-raising flour

2 large eggs, beaten

3 tablespoons milk

2–3 drops vanilla essence and a little mixed spice (optional)

SERVES 10 **Peggy Ellwood donated this recipe for a plain but very good fruit loaf of a type that is well known in the Lake District, in which the dried fruit is soaked in tea before the loaf is mixed.**

1 The night before you want to make the loaf, pour the tea over the dried fruit and leave to soak.

2 Next day, preheat the oven to 170°C, 325°F, Gas mark 3. Liberally grease a 900g (2lb) loaf tin and line it with greaseproof paper or baking parchment.

3 Add all the other ingredients to the soaked dried fruit and mix well together. Pour into the prepared loaf tin.

4 Bake the fruit loaf on the middle shelf of the preheated oven for 1½–2 hours. Leave to cool in the tin before cutting into slices and serving well buttered.

Soak the dried fruit in strong tea before mixing

Honiton Fairings

Also known as brandy snaps, these thin crisp Devonshire biscuits were associated with other fairs in southern England. Eat them alone, fill with whipped cream, or serve with creamy desserts.

MAKES 15

Ingredients

55g (2oz) butter

55g (2oz) demerara sugar

55g (2oz) golden syrup

55g (2oz) plain flour

½ teaspoon ground ginger

1 teaspoon lemon juice

1–2 teaspoons brandy

1 Preheat the oven to 190°C, 375°F, Gas mark 5. Line some baking trays with baking paper or use non-stick ones.

2 Put the butter, sugar and golden syrup in a pan and melt over a low heat. When liquid, gently stir in the flour, ground ginger, lemon juice and brandy.

3 Drop teaspoons of the mixture, widely spaced – the biscuits spread as they cook – on to the baking trays. Cook in the preheated oven for about 5 minutes.

4 Remove from the oven, leave on the trays to cool for a minute and then lift each biscuit with a palette knife and wrap around the handle of a wooden spoon. If the biscuits cool too much, they can be returned to the oven for a moment to soften; or they may be left flat. Leave them to cool completely and then store in an airtight container.

Fill the brandy snaps with whipped cream

Shearing Cake

SERVES 12 **Mrs Ellis, who lives in north Wales, makes this cake every year at sheep-shearing time. She says: 'It was handed down to me from my mother and my grandmother, and it has also been put in Katherine Hepburn's *Stories of My Life*. She was filming at our farm in *The Corn is Green* (1979) and they were doing the tea party scene in the garden and wanted a cake. I was asked if I had a cake, and I gave them my shearing cake, as we were going to shear the sheep the next day. They took it, but ate the lot and I had to make another one. The following day, Katherine Hepburn asked if she could have the recipe as she enjoyed it so much.'**

1 Preheat the oven to 200°C, 400°F, Gas mark 6. Grease a 22cm (8½in) round cake tin and line with greaseproof paper.

2 Rub the butter into the flour. Stir in the currants and caster sugar. Add the eggs and milk and stir well to make a soft, but not runny mixture. Spoon it into the cake tin and sprinkle the top with the brown sugar.

3 Bake in the preheated oven for 15 minutes, then reduce the heat to 170°C, 325°F, Gas mark 3 and bake for another 1¾ hours. Test with a skewer – when the cake is cooked, the skewer will come out clean. Cool in the tin.

Ingredients

340g (12oz) butter, plus extra for greasing

450g (1lb) self-raising flour

340g (12oz) currants

340g (12oz) caster sugar

2 eggs, beaten

200ml (7fl oz) milk

1 tablespoon soft brown sugar

Bara Brith

MAKES 2 **Bara Brith means 'speckled bread' in Welsh, and it is another variation on the fruit bread theme that is so common in Britain. It should be noted that it works better with really good raisins.**

Ingredients

100ml (3½fl oz) milk

a pinch of granulated sugar

1 scant tablespoon yeast

500g (1lb 2oz) strong plain flour, plus extra for dusting

115g (4oz) soft brown sugar

½ teaspoon salt

½ teaspoon mixed spice

115g (4oz) lard or butter, or a mixture of both, plus extra for greasing

170g (6oz) good-quality raisins

170g (6oz) currants

55g (2oz) mixed candied peel, chopped

1 egg, beaten

1 Warm the milk, add a pinch of granulated sugar and the yeast. Mix the flour with the brown sugar, salt and spice, then rub in the fat roughly. Stir in the dried fruit and peel. Add the yeast mixture and the egg and mix to a dough, adding a little more water or milk if necessary. Knead well on a floured surface, then allow to rise until doubled in size – this may take 2 hours.

2 Knock back the dough, divide into 2 pieces and shape each one into a loaf. Place in two 1.2 litre (2 pint) greased loaf tins and leave to prove until well risen.

3 Bake the loaves in a preheated oven at 200°C, 400°F, Gas mark 6 for 15 minutes, then lower the heat to 180°C, 350°F, Gas mark 4 and cook for a further 40–45 minutes, or until the loaves sound hollow when they are tapped underneath with your knuckles. They are best kept for a couple of days before cutting. Serve sliced and buttered.

Use really good raisins for the best results

Barm Brack

Ingredients

1 dessertspoon dried yeast

55ml (2fl oz) warm water

55g (2oz) caster sugar

500g (1lb 2oz) plain flour

1 scant teaspoon salt

15g (½oz) caraway seeds

250ml (9fl oz) hand-hot milk

40g (1½oz) butter, plus extra
for greasing

1 egg, beaten

MAKES 1

This lovely recipe comes with apologies to the contemporary Ulster baking tradition, which now relies on cream of tartar and bicarbonate of soda to raise breads and cakes of all kinds. It dates to 1825, before chemical raising agents were available. No apologies for the results, which are superb.

1 Sprinkle the yeast on to the warm water with a pinch of sugar and set aside until frothy. Mix the flour, the remaining sugar, salt and seeds. Warm the milk to hand-hot and melt the butter in it. Beat in the egg. Mix this into the flour with the yeast mixture to make a dough, adding a little more milk or water if necessary. Knead the dough well, place in a bowl and leave to rise in a warm place for 3 hours.

2 Knock back the dough and place in a greased 20cm (8in) round cake tin. Leave to prove for about 40 minutes, until puffed up and well risen.

3 Bake the loaf in a preheated oven at 200°C, 400°F, Gas mark 6 for 20 minutes, then lower the heat to 180°C, 350°F, Gas mark 4 and bake for a further 15–20 minutes. If the base of the loaf sounds hollow when it is tapped with your knuckles, it is done. Turn out and cool on a wire rack. This is excellent with butter and cheese.

This is excellent with butter and cheese

Ellerbeck Spice Bread

MAKES
1

This recipe for spice bread was collected in the 1930s by Mrs Arthur Webb. Ellerbeck lies on the eastern edge of the Cleveland Hills in Yorkshire.

1 Whisk the yeast into 100ml (3½fl oz) milk with a pinch of sugar and set aside until frothy. Mix the flour, salt, remaining sugar and spice. Rub in the butter – not as thoroughly as for pastry, just until it is well distributed. Make a well in the middle and pour in the yeast mixture. Stir in a little of the flour from around the edge and leave it to work for a further 20 minutes.

2 Mix to a dough, adding the remaining milk as necessary. Knead well, place in an oiled bowl, cover with a damp cloth and leave in a warm place for an hour or so. The mixture is unlikely to rise much.

3 Knock back and knead in the fruit, candied peel and egg. Shape into a loaf and place in a greased and lined 900g (2lb) loaf tin. Leave to prove for an hour — it won't rise very much.

4 Bake the loaf in a preheated oven at 180°C, 350°F, Gas mark 4 for 1 hour 20 minutes – it is ready when a skewer comes out clean – and bake a little longer if necessary. Cool on a wire rack before slicing and spreading with butter.

Ingredients

1 dessertspoon dried yeast

200ml (7fl oz) hand-hot milk

140g (5oz) demerara sugar

310g (11oz) strong plain flour

½ teaspoon salt

1 teaspoon mixed sweet spice

115g (4oz) butter, plus extra for greasing

oil, for greasing

115g (4oz) currants

55g (2oz) sultanas

30g (1oz) mixed candied peel

1 egg, beaten

Oatmeal Soda Bread

MAKES 1 **Oats grow best in cool climates; they used to be the principal cereal crop in Wales and Scotland. They have the most protein (16 per cent) of any grain, and the undoubted success of Scots men and women throughout history is sometimes put down to the consumption of oats in the form of porridge. This oatmeal soda bread is easy to make and is delicious to eat straight from the oven or cold with a salad, pasta or nut roast. Soda bread does not keep well and should be eaten within one or two days.**

Ingredients

30g (1oz) butter, plus extra for greasing

450g (1lb) wholemeal flour, plus extra for dusting

1 teaspoon salt

115g (4oz) fine oatmeal

1½ teaspoons cream of tartar

1 teaspoon bicarbonate of soda

425ml (¾ pint) milk and water mix (half and half)

1 Preheat the oven to 180°C, 350°F, Gas mark 4. Lightly grease a baking sheet or tray.

2 In a large bowl, mix together the flour, salt, oatmeal, cream of tartar and bicarbonate of soda. Using your fingers or in a food processor, rub in the butter until the mixture resembles fine breadcrumbs. Add the milk and water, then mix to a soft dough.

3 Turn out on to a lightly floured surface and knead into a loaf shape or slightly flattened round ball. If you wish, at this stage the surface can be deeply scored with a knife in portions.

4 Place the loaf on the prepared baking sheet and bake in the preheated oven for 30–35 minutes. Eat warm or cold.

Eat this soda bread within one or two days

Rye Bread

Ingredients

1 dessertspoon dried yeast

55ml (2fl oz) warm water

250ml (9fl oz) milk

250g (9oz) rye flour

250g (9oz) wholemeal flour, plus extra for dusting

1 teaspoon salt

30g (1oz) honey

lard, butter or oil, for greasing

MAKES 1

Rye and wheat were grown as a mixed crop, which was known as maslin in the Middle Ages. In this recipe, they make a close-textured bread that tastes good with butter and cheese.

1 Add the yeast to the warm water and leave it to work. Warm the milk. Mix the flours and salt in a bowl and add the honey. When the yeast is frothy, mix all the ingredients together to make a dough and knead well. Don't worry if it's slightly sticky. The ingredients can be mixed in a food processor, in which case they need only a minute to mix.

2 Cover and leave to rise overnight – the dough will be fine left in the kitchen if it is cool; otherwise, you can put it on the top shelf of the refrigerator.

3 Next morning, knock back the dough, lightly flour a work surface and knead it again. Shape into a loaf and put it in a greased 900g (2lb) loaf tin. Leave to prove for about 1 hour in a warm place.

4 Bake in a preheated oven at 200°C, 400°F, Gas mark 6 for 15 minutes, then lower the heat to 190°C, 375°F, Gas mark 5 and bake for another 15 minutes. Turn the loaf out of the tin and return it to the oven, switched off, for a further 10 minutes and then allow to cool on a wire rack.

Kentish Huffkins

MAKES 12 **Small regional breads are still made all over Britain. The recipes vary in their small details and the names are often intriguing. This is the Kent version of fine white bread rolls.**

1 Add the sugar and yeast to the warm milk and set aside for a few minutes until it forms a frothy head. Mix the salt into the flour and rub in the lard. Stir in the yeast mixture and mix to form a dough, adding a little water if necessary.

2 Knead for 10 minutes, then put the dough in an oiled bowl and cover with a damp cloth. Leave to rise in a warm place until doubled in size, for about 1 hour.

3 Knock back the dough and divide into 12 pieces. Roll each one out into an oval about 12cm (5in) long. Place on greased baking trays and make a hole in the centre of each oval. Flour well and prove until the rolls are well risen.

4 Bake in a preheated hot oven at 220°C, 425°F, Gas mark 7 for 15–20 minutes. Wrap the rolls in a warm cloth to preserve the soft crust as they cool.

Ingredients

1 teaspoon granulated sugar

1 dessertspoon dried yeast

250ml (9fl oz) hand-hot milk

½ teaspoon salt

500g (1lb 2oz) strong plain flour, plus extra for dusting

30g (1oz) lard, plus extra for greasing

The Kent version of fine white bread rolls

Wigs

Ingredients

a pinch of caster sugar

100ml (3½fl oz) warm water

2 teaspoons dried yeast

500g (1lb 2oz) strong plain flour

½ teaspoon salt

50g (1¾oz) lard, plus extra
for greasing

50g (1¾oz) soft light brown sugar

1 tablespoon caraway seeds

150ml (5fl oz) milk

MAKES 16 **A 'wig' was the name given to a small bread roll from the late Middle Ages well into the nineteenth century. They were usually a little richer than plain bread, and both Kendal and Hawkshead were noted for them, although they now seem to be forgotten. This is a great shame because they are very good. This recipe from the Lake District was recorded by Florence White.**

1 Add the caster sugar to the warm water, then adt the yeast and leave to work until frothy. Put the flour and salt in a bowl and rub in the lard. Stir in the sugar and caraway seeds. Add the yeast mixture, the milk and a little more water if necessary to make a dough. Knead well, then leave to rise in a warm place.

2 When doubled in size, knock back the dough and divide into 16 pieces. Roll each one into a small, flat round and place on a greased baking tray. Set aside to prove.

3 When the rolls are well risen, bake them in a preheated oven at 180°C, 350°F, Gas mark 4 for 15–20 minutes. Cool on a wire rack. Serve split in half and spread with butter.

Serve these rolls split in half with butter

Teacakes

Ingredients

1 teaspoon dried yeast

about 250ml (9fl oz) tepid water

500g (1lb 2oz) plain flour

30g (1oz) sugar

a pinch of salt

30g (1oz) lard, plus extra
for greasing

30g (1oz) currants

30g (1oz) raisins

MAKES 8

Teacakes are a perennial favourite. This recipe is for a type of little bread that is well known in Yorkshire. Serve hot or toasted with lots of butter.

1 Mix the yeast with 100ml (3½fl oz) tepid water and set aside until frothy. Put the flour, sugar and salt in a bowl and rub in the lard. Add the dried fruit. Pour in the yeast mixture and stir. Add another 100ml (3½fl oz) water and keep mixing to form a dough, adding more water if necessary. Knead well, then cover with a cloth or clingfilm and set aside to rise.

2 When doubled in size, knock back the dough and divide it into 8 pieces. Flatten each one into a disc, about 10–12cm (4–5in) in diameter. Place them on some greased baking trays and set aside to prove.

3 When nicely risen, bake the teacakes in a preheated oven at 220°C, 425°F, Gas mark 7 for 10–15 minutes. Eat warm with butter, or allow to cool, split and toast.

Serve hot or toasted with lots of butter

Norfolk Rusks

MAKES 18 **These little bread rolls are unusual in English bread-making, but they are a well-established recipe in Norfolk. They store well in an airtight tin.**

1 Rub the butter into the flour. Mix in the salt and baking powder. Add the egg and stir well, then add enough milk to make a fairly stiff paste. Divide into 18 pieces and roll each into a round, 1cm (½in) thick.

2 Place on a greased baking sheet and bake in a preheated oven at 220°C, 425°F, Gas mark 7 for 5–7 minutes, until well risen. Remove from the oven and allow to cool for a short time, then score round the middle with a sharp knife and gently pull each one in half.

3 Return to a cool oven at 150°C, 300°F, Gas mark 2 until golden and dry all the way through (this takes about an hour). Cool and store in an airtight container. Eat with butter.

These golden rusks are crisp and dry

Ingredients

100g (3½oz) butter, plus extra for greasing

200g (7oz) plain flour

½ teaspoon salt

1 teaspoon baking powder

1 egg, beaten

2 tablespoons milk

Mrs Ingleby's Oatcakes

Ingredients

300g (10½oz) medium oatmeal

140g (5oz) plain flour

½ teaspoon salt

70g (2½oz) lard or butter

4–5 tablespoons buttermilk
(yoghurt is a good substitute
if this is not available)

MAKES 36

This early twentieth-century recipe for oatcakes comes from Littondale in Yorkshire. Eat them with butter or cheese and some relish or chutney.

1 Put all the dry ingredients in a bowl and rub in the lard or butter with your fingertips. Add the buttermilk or yoghurt and mix to a stiff dough. Press together and cut into 3 equal pieces. Roll each piece out to 5mm (¼in) thick. Slide on to a baking tray (no need to grease) and cut each into 12 sections.

2 Bake the oatcakes in a preheated oven at 180°C, 350°F, Gas mark 4 for about 15 minutes. Leave to cool on a wire rack and then store in an airtight container.

Eat the oatcakes with butter or cheese and chutney

Savoury Cheese and Anchovy Straws

Ingredients

plain flour, for dusting

225g (8oz) puff pastry (see page 300)

30g (1oz) anchovy fillets, drained of oil or washed free from preserving salt

1 egg, separated

100g (3½oz) Cheshire cheese, grated

1 tablespoon chopped fresh parsley

MAKES 16

The idea for these unusual cheese straws came from an important eighteenth-century cookery book, *The Experienced English Housekeeper* (1769), written by Elizabeth Raffald, who for a time was the housekeeper at Arley Hall in Cheshire.

1 Preheat the oven to 220°C, 425°F, Gas mark 7. Lie a baking tray with a sheet of baking paper. Dust a work surface with the flour and roll out the puff pastry into an oblong, about 5mm (¼in) thick. Cut the pastry in half to give 2 equal-sized oblongs.

2 Mash the anchovy fillets to a soft paste with a little egg yolk in a small bowl (do not make the mixture too runny). In another bowl, mix the cheese, parsley and some egg white to make a firm paste (again, you may not need all of the egg).

3 Spread the anchovy paste over one of the oblongs of pastry, right up to the edges. Stack the other pastry oblong on top. Carefully spread the cheese paste evenly over this, again taking it right up to the edges. Cut the pastry sandwich with a sharp knife to give 16 equal-sized fingers. Carefully transfer them to the prepared baking tray, leaving plenty of space around each one (use 2 baking trays, if necessary).

4 Bake in the preheated oven for 5 minutes, then check that the straws are cooking evenly and not scorching – shuffle them around on the baking tray, if necessary. Return to the oven until they are golden; this may take 15–20 minutes, but check frequently. Eat fresh from the oven with drinks, or serve as an accompaniment to soup.

Puddings

Pear Tarts

SERVES 8 **The base for these delicious fruit tarts is made with a rich yeast dough as often used in France. However, if preferred, you can substitute home-made or bought puff or shortcrust pastry.**

Ingredients

plain flour, for dusting

4 large ripe Conference pears, peeled, cored, quartered and thinly sliced

50g (1¾oz) butter

brown sugar, for sprinkling

Yeast pastry

1 teaspoon dried yeast

75ml (2½fl oz) warm water

a pinch of sugar

120ml (4fl oz) single cream

1 whole egg and 1 egg yolk

grated zest of ¼ lemon

250g (9oz) strong plain flour, plus extra for dusting

½ teaspoon salt

butter, for greasing

1 Make the yeast pastry: mix the yeast, water and sugar together in a bowl and set aside until it froths. Beat in the cream, egg, yolk and lemon zest. Put the flour in a large mixing bowl and add the salt. Stir in the yeast mixture and then mix everything well together. The mixture is too sticky to knead, but you should be able to form it into a flat round. Leave in a warm place to rise for 1–1½ hours.

2 Flour your hands and the work surface and divide the yeast dough into 8 pieces. Shape each piece into a thin disc, about 12–15cm (5–6in) in diameter. Divide the sliced pears between the dough circles, arranging them in an attractive fan shape, as shown in the photograph (opposite).

3 Dot the pears with butter and sprinkle with a little brown sugar. Bake the tarts in a preheated oven at 200°C, 400°F, Gas mark 6 for 10 minutes, then reduce the heat to 180°C, 350°F, Gas mark 4 and cook for another 5 minutes, until the dough is crisp and golden brown. Serve the tarts warm, with some cream if desired.

The pastry base is made with a rich yeast dough

Spiced Plum Tart

Ingredients

250g (9oz) plain flour, plus extra for dusting

40g (1½oz) icing sugar

½ teaspoon ground cinnamon

a pinch of mixed spice

a pinch of salt

125g (4½oz) butter

450g (1lb) plums, halved and stoned

4 small apples, peeled, cored and sliced

200g (7oz) caster sugar

beaten egg or milk, to glaze

SERVES 6-8 **A Pembrokeshire farmer's wife contributed this recipe to *Farmhouse Fare*, which was published by the *Farmers Weekly* magazine in 1950.**

1 Mix the flour, icing sugar, cinnamon, mixed spice and salt in a large bowl. Rub in the butter with your fingertips, and then gradually add enough water to make a stiffish dough.

2 Roll out two-thirds of the pastry on a lightly floured surface and use it to line a deep pie dish. Add the plums, apples and sugar. Roll out the remaining pastry to make a lid and use to cover and seal the pie. Glaze the pastry with beaten egg or milk.

3 Bake the tart in a preheated hot oven at 200°C, 400°F, Gas mark 6 for 20 minutes, then turn down the heat to 180°C, 350°F, Gas mark 4 and cook for another 20–25 minutes, until the pastry is crisp and golden brown. Serve hot or cold with cream or ice cream.

Serve hot or cold with cream or ice cream

Gooseberry Pies

These pies are made with a hot-water crust and a hand-raised shell. The recipe and method is local to Oldbury-on-Severn, Gloucestershire, where the pies are still made for summer fêtes and fund-raising events. Traditionally, the edges are nipped up into 21 little points, and the pies themselves are full of gooseberry juice. Make the pies the day before you cook them for the best results.

MAKES 8

Ingredients

500g (1lb 2oz) plain flour

125g (4½oz) butter

125g (4½oz) lard

5 tablespoons boiling water

750g (1lb 10oz) small green gooseberries, topped and tailed

250–310g (9–11oz) demerara sugar

1 Put the flour in a large bowl. Cut the butter and lard into small dice, make a well in the centre of the flour and place the fat in it. Pour the boiling water over and rapidly mix until you have a warm, malleable dough.

2 Divide the dough into 8 pieces and work with one piece at a time; keep the remainder, covered with a cloth, in a warm place to stop it drying out. Take one piece of dough, cut away a quarter of it to make a lid, and roll the rest out into a circle slightly smaller than a saucer.

3 Make a pie case by turning up the edges of the circle by 2cm (¾in) all round, pinching the pastry so that it stands up. Fill with some of the gooseberries and a fairly liberal amount of sugar. Roll the smaller piece of pastry into a circle big enough for a lid, brush with water and use it to cover the berries and sugar, pinching the edges together all round to seal the pie. Repeat with the other pieces of pastry to make 8 pies.

4 Place the pies on baking trays and leave overnight in a cool place for the pastry to set. Bake them in a preheated hot oven at 200–220°C, 400–425°F, Gas mark 6–7 for 25–30 minutes, until crisp and golden brown. Don't worry if some of the juice escapes while cooking – the pies will still taste just as good. Serve them tepid or allow to cool.

Curd Tart

SERVES 8-10 **On farms, this Yorkshire recipe was made using 'beestings' – the first milk a cow gives after calving, which curdles naturally when it is heated. Of course, this is unobtainable unless you happen to have a dairy herd. Alternative methods for making curd include heating milk with eggs or Epsom salts or using rennet, as in the method given here.**

Ingredients

1 litre (1¾ pints) whole milk

rennet

225g (8oz) shortcrust pastry made with butter (see page 298)

plain flour, for dusting

50g (1¾oz) butter

100g (3½oz) caster sugar

grated zest of 1 lemon

1 egg

50g (1¾oz) currants

50g (1¾oz) mixed candied peel

1 tablespoon rum

nutmeg, for grating

1 The night before you want to make the tart, heat the milk to blood temperature and add the rennet, according to the packet instructions. When the curd has set and cooled, put it into a square of clean muslin and hang it above a bowl to drain overnight – it must be well drained.

2 The next day, roll out the pastry on a lightly floured surface and use to line a 20cm (8in) round pie dish or tart tin. Cream the butter, sugar and lemon zest together. Beat in the egg. Mash the curd with a fork, and stir into the mixture. Add the currants, candied peel and rum and pour into the pastry case.

3 Bake the curd tart in a preheated moderate oven at 190°C, 375°F, Gas mark 5 for about 40 minutes, or until the filling is set. Grate a little nutmeg over the top while it is still warm.

Grate some nutmeg over the warm pie

East Anglian Treacle Custard Tart

Ingredients

plain flour, for dusting

450g (1lb) shortcrust pastry made with butter (see page 298)

200g (7oz) golden syrup

30g (1oz) butter

grated zest and juice of 1 lemon

2 eggs, beaten

SERVES 8 **This sweet and addictive dessert was recorded by Florence White as a dish from East Anglia. It is a delicious variation on the more familiar treacle tart, which is made with breadcrumbs (see page 242).**

1 Roll out the pastry on a lightly floured surface and use it to line an 18–20cm (7–8in) round tart tin. Cover the pastry with greaseproof paper, fill with dried baking beans and then 'bake blind' for 15 minutes in a preheated moderate oven at 180°C, 350°F, Gas mark 4. Remove the paper and beans and return to the oven for another 5 minutes.

2 Put the golden syrup and butter in a pan over a gentle heat. When the butter has melted, remove the pan from the heat and add the lemon juice and zest. Beat in the eggs, mixing well between each addition.

3 Pour into the pastry case and bake in a preheated slow oven at 150°C, 300°F, Gas mark 2 for 30–35 minutes, until the filling is just set in the middle. Serve cool but not chilled.

Serve this tart cool rather than chilled

Anne Horne's Butter Tart

SERVES 10

Also sometimes known as Border Tart, there are numerous variations of this traditional north-eastern favourite. All are very sweet – treats for people who worked long days outside in the cold.

1 Roll out the shortcrust pastry on a lightly floured surface and use it to line a 23cm (9in) round flan dish.

2 Mix together the melted butter, dried fruit, sugar, beaten eggs and vanilla essence and pour into the pastry case.

3 Bake in a preheated hot oven at 200°C, 400°F, Gas mark 6 for 30–40 minutes. Serve the tart warm with whipped cream.

Ingredients

450g (1lb) shortcrust pastry made with butter (see page 298)

plain flour, for dusting

85g (3oz) butter, melted

300g (10½oz) currants or mixed fruit

300g (10½oz) demerara sugar

3 eggs, beaten

2–3 drops vanilla essence

There are many variations of this traditional sweet tart

Treacle Tart

SERVES 8 **Although this traditional dessert uses golden syrup, it has always been known as treacle tart. This Yorkshire recipe is a more elaborate version of the simple syrup-and-breadcrumb concoctions that most of us knew when we were children.**

Ingredients

225g (8oz) shortcrust pastry made with butter and lard mixed (see page 298)

plain flour, for dusting

50g (1¾oz) currants

50g (1¾oz) sultanas

50g (1¾oz) mixed candied peel, chopped

55g (2oz) fresh brown breadcrumbs

1 apple, peeled and grated

a pinch of ground ginger

a pinch of mixed spice

2 generous tablespoons golden syrup, warmed

grated zest and juice of 1 lemon

1 Roll out the pastry on a lightly floured surface and use to line an 18cm (7in) round tart tin.

2 Scatter the currants, sultanas and peel over the pastry base. Mix together the breadcrumbs, grated apple, ground spices, golden syrup and lemon zest and juice, then spoon over the dried fruit, levelling the top neatly.

3 Bake in a preheated hot oven at 200°C, 400°F, Gas mark 6 for 20 minutes, then lower the temperature to 180°C, 350°F, Gas mark 4 and continue cooking for a further 10 minutes. Serve the tart warm with cream or custard.

Serve the treacle tart warm
with cream or custard

Cherry Bumpers

MAKES 6 **These delicious individual pies are a variation on the more familiar cherry turnovers. They are traditional to Buckinghamshire, where cherries were once an important fruit crop.**

Ingredients

450g (1lb) shortcrust pastry made with butter and lard mixed (see page 298)

plain flour, for dusting

1 tablespoon ground almonds

2 tablespoons caster sugar, plus extra for sprinkling

1 drop bitter almond essence

250g (9oz) fresh cherries, stoned

butter, for greasing

1 Roll out the pastry fairly thinly on a lightly floured surface and cut out six 10–12cm (4–5in) circles.

2 Mix the ground almonds with 2 tablespoons of caster sugar and work a drop of almond essence through the mixture with your fingers. Put a little of this almond mixture in the centre of each pastry circle, then divide the cherries between them.

3 Brush round the edge of each pastry circle with a little cold water and then crimp the edges firmly to enclose the filling. Lightly brush the top of each little parcel with water and then sprinkle with caster sugar.

4 Place the cherry bumpers on a greased baking tray and bake in a preheated hot oven at 200°C, 400°F, Gas mark 6 for 12–15 minutes. Eat warm – but be careful when they are fresh from the oven as the cherries become very hot – or cold.

A variation on the more familiar cherry turnovers

Sutton Wakes Pudding

SERVES 4-6 **This Peak District recipe is like a hot version of summer pudding. A 'wake' was originally a vigil or watch that was observed to honour the local parish's patron saint. Progressing from an overnight vigil, the 'wake' eventually became a celebration or fair, sometimes lasting up to a week.**

1 Mix the flour and breadcrumbs together. Using the coarse side of a grater, grate the cold butter into the mixture and distribute as evenly as possible. Add enough cold water, a tablespoon at a time, to make a firm dough.

2 Grease a 1.2 litre (2 pint) pudding basin with a little softened butter and sprinkle lightly with demerara sugar. Roll out the dough and use it to line the basin, reserving a quarter to make a lid. Add the fruit in layers, scattering caster sugar in between each one. Roll out the remaining pastry into a circle, dampen the edges and place it over the filling, sealing well. Trim off any excess, cover with a double layer of foil and tie on firmly with string, making a loop over the top as a handle.

3 Place in a large pan and add boiling water to come halfway up the sides of the basin. Steam gently for 2 hours, adding more boiling water as and when necessary.

4 You can try unmoulding this pudding, but use a deep dish, as lots of juice will flow out of it, and you must be prepared for it to collapse. It's much safer to serve it straight from the bowl. Serve it hot with some cold thick cream.

Ingredients

140g (5oz) self-raising flour

100g (3½oz) fine fresh white breadcrumbs

100g (3½oz) salted butter, well chilled, plus softened butter for greasing

demerara sugar, for sprinkling

750g (1lb 10oz) mixed soft fruit, such as blackcurrants, strawberries, raspberries, redcurrants, gooseberries or rhubarb

85g (3oz) caster sugar

Bakewell Pudding

Ingredients

*250g (9oz) puff pastry
(ready-made pastry is fine)*

plain flour, for dusting

100–140g (3½–5oz) raspberry jam

4 egg yolks

100g (3½oz) butter, melted

100g (3½oz) caster sugar

100g (3½oz) ground almonds

1 drop bitter almond essence

2 egg whites

SERVES 6 **This delicious version of a perennial favourite was recorded by the children's author Alison Uttley, who grew up in Derbyshire not far from Bakewell. It's a lovely, rich dish for special occasions.**

1 Roll out the puff pastry thinly on a lightly floured surface and use it to line a deep oval ovenproof dish, about 850ml (1½ pints). Trim the edges neatly and spread a generous layer of jam over the bottom.

2 Mix together the egg yolks, melted butter, sugar, ground almonds and almond essence. Beat the egg whites to a froth and gently stir into the mixture in a figure-of-eight movement with a metal spoon.

3 Bake the pudding in a preheated moderate oven at 180°C, 350°F, Gas mark 4 for about 40 minutes. Serve tepid.

*A lovely, rich dish
for special occasions*

Steamed Ginger Sponge Pudding

Ingredients

115g (4oz) butter, plus extra
for greasing

115g (4oz) caster sugar

2 eggs

170g (6oz) self-raising flour

55g (2oz) preserved stem ginger,
finely chopped

3 tablespoons golden syrup

Ginger sauce

300ml (½ pint) full cream milk

1 tablespoon grated fresh root
ginger

30g (1oz) butter

30g (1oz) plain flour

55g (2oz) caster sugar

SERVES 4 **This delicious, warming recipe is from Cornwall. The light, spicy sponge pudding is served with a hot ginger sauce. You can add cream or custard if you are feeling really decadent.**

1 Butter an 850ml (1½ pint) pudding basin. Cream together the butter and sugar until pale and fluffy. Beat in the eggs, adding one spoonful of flour with each egg, then fold in the remaining flour and the chopped stem ginger.

2 Drizzle the syrup into the bottom of the basin, then spoon the pudding mixture over the top. Smooth the top of the pudding and cover with a layer of greaseproof paper and one of foil. Place in a steamer or a saucepan and add boiling water to come halfway up the sides of the basin. Steam for 1–1½ hours, adding more boiling water as and when necessary.

3 While the pudding is steaming, make the sauce. Bring the milk to the boil with the ginger. Let the mixture stand for at least 30 minutes to infuse, then strain off the milk. Melt the butter slowly and stir in the flour. Cook gently for 2–3 minutes and then add the milk gradually, stirring all the time. Bring the sauce to the boil and simmer for at least 5 minutes, stirring constantly. Add the sugar and stir until dissolved.

4 Turn out the pudding and cut into quarters. Pass the sauce round separately. Serve both warm – there is no need to burn tongues – the gentle spiciness will add its own heat.

Apple Pancakes with Cider Sauce

Ingredients

2–3 large, well-flavoured apples, peeled, cored and sliced

100g (3½oz) plain flour

a pinch of salt

2 eggs

1 tablespoon rum

250ml (9fl oz) milk

50g (1¾oz) butter, plus extra for frying the pancakes

50g (1¾oz) demerara sugar

300ml (½ pint) cider

SERVES 6 **This pudding was influenced by the cider and apple tradition of the south-west of England. Cider-makers sometimes give their products extra flavour by storing them in barrels formerly used for fortified wine or spirits. Why not use a Devon cider that has been kept in a rum barrel if you can get one?**

1 Put the apples in a saucepan with 1 tablespoon water and cook very gently over a low heat until soft.

2 Mix the flour and salt and beat in the eggs, then beat in the rum and milk until you have a smooth batter.

3 Heat a small frying pan and add a tiny piece of butter. When it melts, add a little batter and swirl it around to cover the bottom. Cook over a medium heat, until set and golden brown underneath. Flip it over and cook the other side. Repeat with the remaining batter to make 12 thin pancakes.

4 Spread each pancake with a little of the apple purée, roll up and arrange in a heatproof dish. Place in a preheated low oven at 170°C, 325°F, Gas mark 3 for 5–10 minutes to warm the pancakes and crisp the edges slightly.

5 Meanwhile, melt the butter in a saucepan and stir in the sugar. Add the cider, bring to the boil and cook rapidly until the mixture has reduced by at least half and is slightly syrupy. Serve hot with the pancakes.

Caramelised Baked Pumpkin

SERVES 4-6 **Mr Upton began gardening at Slindon Estate in West Sussex in the 1950s. As he was unable to interest anyone in the traditional apple varieties growing there, he began cultivating pumpkins and squashes instead. This unusual recipe works really well with any variety.**

Ingredients

1kg (2lb 3oz) pumpkin

30g (1oz) butter

salt and pepper

2 tablespoons demerara sugar

1 Cut the peel off the pumpkin, and then remove and discard the seeds and the stringy centre. Cut the orange pumpkin flesh into rough cubes.

2 Melt the butter in a shallow flameproof dish. Add the pumpkin and turn it in the butter so that it is well coated. Sprinkle with salt, pepper and demerara sugar.

3 Bake the pumpkin in a preheated hot oven at 240°C, 475°F, Gas mark 9 for 15 minutes, then reduce the heat to 220°C, 425°F, Gas mark 7 for a further 10 minutes, or until the pumpkin is tender but not mushy. Serve immediately with cream.

Serve the pumpkin with lashings of cream

Gingerbread and Raspberry Crumble

Ingredients

140g (5oz) butter

250g (9oz) self-raising flour

115g (4oz) soft light brown sugar

1 teaspoon ground ginger

½ teaspoon grated lemon zest

500g (1lb 2oz) fresh raspberries

SERVES 6 **The short-textured zesty gingerbread of the style associated with Grasmere also makes an excellent crumble-type pudding, such as this one from the Lake District. We have used raspberries but you can substitute almost any summer berries or stone fruits, such as plums, greengages and apricots.**

1 Using your fingertips, gently rub the butter into the flour, until it resembles fine breadcrumbs. Stir in the sugar, ground ginger and lemon zest.

2 Put the raspberries in a deep baking dish. Cover the fruit with the crumble mixture, but don't press it down.

3 Bake in a preheated moderate oven at 180°C, 350°F, Gas mark 4 for 30 minutes, until golden brown and crisp on top. Cool the crumble a little before serving tepid with thick cream.

Substitute almost any summer berries or stone fruits

Mrs Palmer's Russian Cream

Ingredients

500ml (18fl oz) full-fat milk

2 eggs, separated

100g (3½oz) caster sugar

a few drops vanilla essence or a little grated lemon zest

1 sachet powdered gelatine

SERVES 6 **Gillian Palmer, from Lanteglos near Fowey in Cornwall, remarks that this recipe was 'a great favourite' with the teams of men who followed the threshing machines around the farms in the early twentieth century. Similar dishes have been made in Britain since at least the eighteenth century, but they don't seem to have much to do with Russia. It's well worth experimenting with different flavourings. Try a little lemon zest or vanilla essence.**

1 Put the milk in a saucepan. Add the egg yolks, caster sugar and some flavouring, if used, and sprinkle the gelatine over the top. Stir thoroughly to break up the egg yolks and distribute the gelatine well, then place over a low heat. Meanwhile, whisk the egg whites to a stiff foam.

2 Increase the heat and bring just to the boil, stirring all the time (don't worry if it shows signs of curdling). Remove the pan from the heat and stir the beaten egg whites through the mixture. Turn into a bowl and leave overnight in a cool place.

3 To serve, put a plate over the bowl, invert and shake gently. The pudding should slide out, and will have a clear jelly layer and a foamy layer. Serve with clotted cream.

Raspberry Cream

**SERVES
4-6**

This dessert is based on a recipe from a cookery manuscript dated 1847, which belongs to the National Trust. It is especially good when made with rich, thick cream from the West Country.

1 Set aside a few of the nicest raspberries for decoration. Rub the rest of the fruit through a sieve to make a purée.

2 Mix the raspberry purée with the sugar and brandy and put about a tablespoon of this into the bottom of each of 4–6 individual serving glasses.

3 Add the cream to the remaining purée and beat until stiff. Spoon into the glasses on top of the purée. Decorate with mint sprigs and the reserved whole raspberries. Chill in the refrigerator before serving.

Ingredients

340g (12oz) raspberries

70g (2½oz) caster sugar

2 tablespoons brandy

250ml (9fl oz) double cream

mint sprigs, to decorate

Decorate with mint sprigs and raspberries

Gooseberries with Elderberry Zabaglione

Ingredients

300g (10½oz) gooseberries

4 egg yolks

4 tablespoons granulated sugar

4 tablespoons elderflower cordial

1 tablespoon vodka (optional)

SERVES 4 **Most country people used to grow gooseberries – they were low-maintenance and provided home-grown fruit early in the summer. It's hard to beat a traditional gooseberry fool (cooked, crushed berries, custard and whipped cream), but sometimes it's nice to have a change, as in this unusual recipe. Although you can make the purée in advance, the zabaglione is a last-minute task.**

1 Put the gooseberries in a pan with just enough water to cover the bottom. Cook gently until soft, then sieve. Chill the purée in the refrigerator until you are ready to serve the dessert.

2 Just before serving, divide the purée between 4 individual serving dishes or glasses.

3 Put the egg yolks and sugar in a bowl and beat with a whisk until pale yellow. Add the elderflower cordial and vodka, if using. Place the bowl over a pan of simmering water (don't let it touch the water, or it will curdle) and keep beating until the mixture is thick and foamy.

4 Divide the zabaglione between the dishes or glasses and serve immediately, perhaps with some little almond biscuits.

Make the zabaglione at the last minute

Plums and Cream

SERVES 4-6 **Fruit was often just stewed and served with custard or cream to make simple puddings in Kent, the garden of England. This version is good made with purple Early Rivers plums, developed by Thomas Rivers in the nineteenth century.**

Ingredients

500g (1lb 2oz) plums

200g (7oz) sugar

150ml (¼ pint) water

1 vanilla pod, split lengthways

sour cream or crème fraîche, to serve

1 Put the plums, sugar, water and vanilla pod in a saucepan and cook very gently over a low heat, until the plums are tender but not mushy. Remove the vanilla pod.

2 At this point, you can either leave the plums whole or make a slightly more complex and elegant dish by coarsely sieving them or putting them through a mouli-légumes. If you do this, take a dozen plum stones, break them and add the kernels to the purée. Chill well and serve in glasses with a good spoonful of sour cream or crème fraîche in each.

Stewed Pears

SERVES 6 **This delicious variation on pears in red wine was traditionally made in September, the time of the Barnstaple Fair in Devon.**

Ingredients

6 medium pears, peeled, cored and sliced

340g (12oz) granulated sugar

zest and juice of 1 lemon

100ml (3½fl oz) port

3–4 cloves

about 500ml (18fl oz) water

1 drop cochineal

slivered almonds, toasted

1 Put the pears in a saucepan with the sugar, lemon zest and juice, port, cloves and enough water to cover them. Add a drop of cochineal, if you want them to be really pink.

2 Simmer gently for about 20 minutes, or until the pears are tender. Cool, then place in a serving dish and decorate with the almonds. Serve chilled with single cream.

Hatted Kit

SERVES 6 **This old-fashioned Scottish dish of curds was eclipsed by the popularity of yoghurt. The original ingredients were buttermilk from the churn and a cow, to be milked directly into the buttermilk – both now presenting difficulties unless you actually happen to own a cow. An approximation is possible with cultured buttermilk, but it needs a little help.**

Ingredients

500ml (18fl oz) buttermilk

juice of ½ lemon

500ml (18fl oz) whole milk

1 Put the buttermilk and lemon juice in a pan and heat to blood heat. Pour into a large jug or bowl. Put the milk in the pan (there is no need to rinse it in between) and heat this to blood heat as well. Pour into the warm buttermilk in a thin stream, whisking the mixture as you do so. Cover and leave overnight at cool room temperature.

2 The following morning, the mixture should have separated into a thick curd (the 'hat') on top of thin whey. Line a sieve with a piece of scalded butter muslin and place over a bowl. Pour the mixture in and leave to drain for 4–5 hours. Discard the whey and store the curds in a covered bowl in the fridge.

3 They can be eaten as a savoury spread on brown bread with a little salt, or as a dessert with caster sugar. The sweetened version was traditionally sprinkled with a little grated nutmeg or powdered cinnamon, either of which are good. Or it can be served with soft fruit, such as raspberries.

Serve with sugar, spices or soft fruit

259

Rhubarb and Stem Ginger Fool

Ingredients

565g (1¼lb) forced rhubarb

100g (3½oz) light brown sugar

250ml (9fl oz) whipping cream

4–5 pieces of preserved stem ginger, in syrup, drained

SERVES 4 **This traditional dessert needs the bright pink early-season rhubarb that is grown in special forcing sheds south of Wakefield in Yorkshire.**

1 Trim off the leaves and bases of the rhubarb stems, then wash the stalks and cut into 2cm (¾in) lengths. Place in an ovenproof dish and add the sugar.

2 Cover the dish and then bake in a preheated moderate oven at 170°C, 325°F, Gas mark 3 for about 30–40 minutes. Set aside to cool before serving.

3 Whip the cream until it is thick but not stiff, then using a metal spoon, gently fold it into the cool rhubarb mixture. Thinly slice the stem ginger and stir into the fool, reserving a few pieces for decoration. Chill in the refrigerator before spooning into individual glasses or dishes. Decorate with the reserved stem ginger and serve.

Only use the bright pink early-season rhubarb

Blackberry Jellies

Ingredients

750g (1lb 10oz) blackberries

1 vanilla pod

1 sachet powdered gelatine

115g (4oz) granulated sugar

*additional blackberries,
to decorate*

SERVES 4-6 **Blackberries grow everywhere in Britain and can be harvested for free in fields and on roadsides. They are used for all sorts of crumbles, pies and puddings as well as preserves.**

1 Rinse the blackberries and put them in a pan with the vanilla pod. Cover tightly and cook gently for a few minutes, until they have yielded all their juice.

2 Strain the juice through a jelly bag. Discard the pulp and measure out the juice. Make up to 500ml (18fl oz) with water if the quantity is a little short. Don't forget to retrieve and rinse the vanilla pod to re-use another day.

3 Put the juice in a pan and heat gently until almost boiling. Pour 100ml (3½fl oz) of the juice into a cup or small bowl and add the gelatine, stirring to dissolve the powder. Add the sugar to the remaining juice and continue to stir until this, too, has dissolved. Remove the pan from the heat and stir in the gelatine mixture.

4 Pour into a large serving dish or individual glasses, or rinse a jelly mould in cold water and pour in the mixture. Leave in the refrigerator until set and serve the jellies chilled, decorated with a few whole blackberries.

Chill the jellies in the refrigerator until set

Little Summer Fruit Moulds

Ingredients

900g (2lb) prepared fresh soft fruit, such as blackcurrants and redcurrants, stripped from their stems; strawberries; blackberries; raspberries; gooseberries, topped and tailed

12 thick slices milk loaf

565ml (1 pint) water

sugar

4 tablespoons cassis or elderflower cordial

Decoration

extra fruit

fresh mint or lemon balm sprigs

SERVES 6 **These moulds are essentially individual summer puddings. Mixing the bread and fruit together makes them firmer and easier to turn out. Try to use at least two varieties of soft fruit.**

1 Put a small piece of baking paper, cut to size, in the bottom of each of 6 individual ramekin dishes.

2 Remove the crusts from the bread and cut into large dice. Put the fruit in a pan, cover with water and simmer until tender. Gooseberries and blackcurrants need 5 minutes whereas strawberries, blackberries and raspberries just need to come to the boil and then be removed from the heat immediately.

3 Remove the fruit from the juice with a slotted spoon and add sufficient sugar to the juice to make a syrup. This will vary according to the fruits and their natural sweetness. Bring the syrup to the boil and simmer for 5 minutes. Allow to cool, then add the cassis or elderflower cordial.

4 Mix the fruit and bread together. Put a little syrup in the bottom of each ramekin, then pack in the fruit and bread, pressing the mixture down well. Spoon more syrup over the top and chill in the refrigerator until required.

5 To serve, carefully run a knife around the inside of each ramekin and unmould on to a dessert plate. Take off the paper, pour the rest of the juice over and then decorate with more fresh fruit and fresh mint or lemon balm sprigs.

Junket

SERVES 6 **Simple and good, this recipe is much nicer in individual dishes than as one large bowlful. This version is sometimes called Devon junket.**

Ingredients

500ml (18fl oz) creamy Channel Islands milk

1 heaped dessertspoon caster sugar

2 tablespoons brandy

rennet

caster sugar, ground cinnamon and clotted cream (optional), to serve

1 Heat the milk to blood heat. Dissolve the sugar in it, and stir in the brandy. Consult the packet instructions for the rennet and stir in the correct amount.

2 Quickly divide the mixture between 6 individual glasses or dishes and leave to set in the refrigerator or a cool place.

3 Just before serving, add a teaspoon of sugar and a dusting of cinnamon to the top of each portion. Add a little clotted cream for a really rich version.

Add a little clotted cream for a really rich junket

Clotted Cream and Blackberry Ripple Ice Cream

SERVES 6 **This ice cream is best made in an electric ice-cream maker, but you will still obtain good results if you make it by hand and use your freezer.**

1 Cook the blackberries gently until they have yielded their juice. Rub through a sieve. Measure 150ml (¼ pint) of juice, then mix in the sugar and bring to the boil. Allow to cool.

2 For the custard, put the milk and half the sugar in a pan and heat to almost boiling. Beat the egg yolks with the remaining sugar until pale and it holds its shape when a ribbon of mix is trailed across the surface. Pour the hot milk in a steady stream on to the egg and sugar mixture, beating steadily. Place the bowl over a pan of simmering water and stir until thickened. When it coats the back of a wooden spoon and holds a horizontal line drawn across the spoon, it is thick enough. Plunge the base of the bowl into cold water to stop it cooking further. Stir in the clotted cream. Cool, stirring occasionally, then chill in the fridge.

3 To freeze in an electric ice-cream machine, churn the cream mix for 10 minutes (no longer, or it will become buttery), and scrape into a plastic freezer box. Add the blackberry and sugar mixture and marble it through the semi-frozen ice cream. Place in the freezer for an hour. Alternatively, put the cream mix in a freezer box, cover and freeze for an hour, scrape the edge to the centre of the mixture and beat for a few seconds with an electric hand beater. Return to the freezer. Repeat after another hour. Marble the blackberry mixture through and freeze until set.

4 Remove from the freezer and give the ice about 15 minutes to soften before serving if it has been frozen solid.

Ingredients

500g (1lb 2oz) blackberries

140g (5oz) sugar

Custard

375ml (13fl oz) milk

115g (4oz) granulated sugar

5 egg yolks

120ml (4fl oz) clotted cream

Cambridge Cheese

Ingredients

1.5 litres (2½ pints) whole milk

100ml (3½fl oz) whipping cream

100ml (3½fl oz) full-fat crème fraîche

1 teaspoon rennet

Making and selling cheese was one way a farmer's wife generated income for herself. Few traditional British recipes for cheese are suitable for making in urban settings in which the ingredients have to be purchased, but this version, which was used in the Fens to the east of Cambridge until the mid-twentieth century, can be made quickly, in small quantities, and tastes delicious. Make it in summer, when the weather is settled and warm.

Crème fraîche will give a slight sourness when relying on pasteurised milk, and imitates a natural souring that develops in unpasteurised milk, or which is induced by cheese-makers with 'starters' of specially cultured bacteria.

You will need a deep metal or plastic tray, a solid wood or plastic board to fit inside it, a sushi mat and some moulds. Traditionally, oblong wooden moulds were used. However, now that the country craftsmen who used to make such objects have all disappeared, you will have to improvise. Some 850ml (1½ pint) foil pudding moulds work quite well, even if the end result is not a traditional shape. Punch 8–10 evenly spaced holes, 5mm (¼in) in diameter, round the sides of each mould. The whole process of making the cheese takes around 3 days.

It takes around three days to make these rich cheeses

1 Start the cheese first thing in the morning. Wash the tray, board, sushi mat and moulds thoroughly with boiling water. Don't add any detergent, as it can taint the cheese. Put the board on the tray, cover with the mat, and have the moulds ready.

2 Mix the milk, cream and crème fraîche in a bowl and then pour into a large saucepan and heat to blood temperature, (think baby milk temperature). Pour the mixture back into the bowl, add the rennet and stir a few times. Then leave it strictly alone for 30 minutes.

3 Press the top gently with a clean finger: it should have set to a firm junket. Carefully spoon this curd into the moulds, dividing it equally between them. Lots of whey will flow out of the moulds in the first few hours – don't worry, this is quite normal – carefully empty it off.

4 Cover the moulds with a clean cloth and leave them for 2–3 days, occasionally checking the amount of whey and emptying the tray if and when necessary. If you have a clean tray, carefully move the board carrying the moulds into it and wash the first one – cleanliness is essential with soft cheeses.

5 At the end of 3 days, unmould the little cheeses; they should have a slightly acid taste and a delicious rich texture. Since they are unsalted, they can be served either with fruit and sugar as a dessert, or with salad and biscuits as a light lunch or starter. Keep refrigerated and eat within 2–3 days.

Jams and Preserves

Strawberry and Redcurrant Jam

Ingredients

500g (1lb 2oz) redcurrants

500g (1lb 2oz) strawberries

500g (1lb 2oz) granulated sugar

Adding some redcurrant juice to the strawberries produces a better set and intensifies the flavour of the jam without being too obvious.

1 Begin the day before you plan to make the jam by placing the redcurrants in a pan; put the lid on and cook over a very gentle heat until they have collapsed and yielded all their juice. Remove from the heat and pour the fruit into a jelly bag that has been suspended over a bowl to catch the juice. Let it drip through – there should be about 200ml (7fl oz).

2 The next day, hull the strawberries, remove any bad bits, and rinse them; halve or quarter any large ones. Place in a large preserving pan with the sugar and the redcurrant juice and heat gently, stirring to dissolve the sugar. Once this is done, bring to the boil and cook for about 15–20 minutes.

3 Test by dropping a teaspoonful on to a chilled saucer. If the jam crinkles when it is lightly pushed with a finger, it's set. When the setting point is reached, remove the pan from the heat, pour into warm, sterilised jars and seal immediately. This makes approximately 1.4–1.8kg (3–4lb) jam.

Cherry Conserve

Ingredients

900g (2lb) dark red cherries

juice and zest of 2 lemons

800g (1¾lb) jam sugar with pectin

2–3 tablespoons cherry brandy or Kirsch (optional)

'Take the best and fairest of cherries' begins the receipt from 1685, on which this recipe is based. Cherries will always be precious. Cherry conserve is very special, and the addition of alcohol turns it into a luxury. Cherries are relatively low in pectin, so the availability of pectin sugar today takes the guesswork out of achieving a set. But even with pectin, don't expect a firm set – this is a runny treat.

1 Stone the cherries and place them with the lemon juice and zest in a large, heavy-based preserving pan. Simmer very gently for about 15 minutes, or until really soft, stirring from time to time to prevent them sticking.

2 Add the sugar and stir over a low heat until it has completely dissolved. Increase the heat and then boil rapidly until setting point is reached (approximately another 5 minutes). Test by dropping a teaspoonful on to a chilled saucer. If the jam crinkles when it is lightly pushed with a finger, it's set.

3 Stir in the alcohol of your choice, if you wish, then ladle the hot jam into warm, sterilised jars and cover when cold with waxed discs and cellophane secured with rubber bands. This makes approximately 1.4–1.8kg (3–4lb) jam.

Cherries are low in pectin, so use jam sugar

Apple Butter

Ingredients

750g (1lb 10oz) apples – a mixture of crab apples and Cox's works well

500g (1lb 2oz) granulated sugar

grated zest and juice of ½ lemon

This old-fashioned preserve could be made from any variety of apple, but particularly sour crab apples. This lovely recipe, from Somerset, makes only a small amount but you can double up the quantities and use a preserving pan if making larger amounts.

1 Wash the apples, quarter them and cut out any unsound bits, but don't peel. Put them in a large pan, add enough cold water to cover them and simmer gently until soft and pulpy (this can take some time with crab apples).

2 Sieve them and measure the pulp; this quantity should yield about 850ml (1½ pints). Return it to the pan and cook gently for an hour until quite thick, stirring from time to time.

3 Add the sugar, lemon zest and juice and boil rapidly until thick and no longer runny, which will take about 20 minutes. Stir constantly and make sure the mixture doesn't catch and burn – you may want to wrap your hand in a tea towel, as the mixture spits as it thickens.

4 Pour into shallow containers and cover when cold. This makes approximately 1kg (2lb 3oz) apple butter.

Use crab apples in this traditional apple butter

Marmalade

Orange marmalade became something of a Scottish speciality, both made at home and commercialised by Keiller's of Dundee. Was it something to do with the cheerful colour and delicious smell it makes in the house during the chill dark days of January? The formula below is based on a recipe in the *Scottish Women's Rural Institute Cookery Book*. It makes a transparent jelly marmalade with a generous quantity of 'chips' of orange peel suspended in it.

Ingredients

Seville (bitter or marmalade) oranges

lemons (unwaxed)

granulated sugar

water

1 Weigh the oranges, and for every 1kg (2lb 3oz) of oranges, add 1 lemon to the scale pan. Make a note of the total weight of fruit used. During the final boiling, you will need to add the equivalent weight of sugar, and half the weight of water.

2 Wash the fruit, put it (whole) into a large pan and cover with water. Bring to the boil and simmer gently until soft. Test from time to time (the old test was to try to push the head of a pin though the skin – if this was easy, then the fruit was done). Lemons soften quicker than oranges, and the time the latter take will vary. Remove them individually to a bowl as they soften enough. Discard the cooking water.

3 Cut the fruit in half and scrape out the pulp into a jelly bag and allow all the juice to run through. Squeeze the bag to collect as much juice as possible, then discard the pulp (or cook it with an equal weight of sugar to make a paste marmalade). Cut the peel of the fruit into thin slivers.

4 Put the slivers of peel and the juice into a preserving pan, add the sugar and water weighed according to the original weight of fruit and bring to the boil, stirring until all the sugar has dissolved. Boil rapidly to setting point, testing after about 15 minutes. Drop a teaspoonful on to a chilled saucer. If the jam crinkles when it is lightly pushed with a finger, it's set. Pot in warm, sterilised jars, cover and seal when cold.

Trelissick Lemon Curd

Ingredients

finely grated zest and juice of 2 large lemons, preferably unwaxed and organic

4 large eggs, lightly beaten

170g (6oz) caster sugar

115g (4oz) unsalted butter, melted

This recipe uses a slow cooker, but we have also given instructions for those of you who don't have one. Lemon curd should be kept in the fridge and eaten within a month or so of making. If your curd curdles while you are making it, don't worry: just remove it quickly from the heat and stand it over a basin of cold water. Whisk hard until the curdling disappears and then continue as before.

1 Place the lemon zest and juice in a basin or dish that will fit in the slow cooker. Add the beaten eggs, sugar and melted butter and stir well. Cover with a piece of foil and place in the slow cooker. Pour enough boiling water into the slow cooker to come halfway up the basin or dish, then cover with the lid of the slow cooker. Cook for about 1½–2 hours, until thick. Stir well with a wooden or plastic spoon (metal implements spoil the flavour), then pot in warm, sterilised jars.

2 If you do not have a slow cooker, follow this method: put the lemon zest and juice in a heatproof basin set over a pan of barely simmering water. Take care not to let the base of the bowl touch the water. Add the well-beaten eggs, sugar and melted butter. Stir the mixture frequently with a wooden or plastic spoon for about 20 minutes, or until thick. Pot in warmed sterilised jars. This quantity makes approximately 3 jars.

Blackberry Curd

A delicious preserve from Wales, based on the same principle as lemon curd (see page 280). This is a good way of using and preserving the wild blackberries that grow so prolifically in our hedgerows during the autumn. It's very satisfying to pick them yourself and then use them to make this blackberry curd.

Ingredients

500g (1lb 2oz) blackberries

140g (5oz) apple, peeled and cored

juice of 1 lemon

600g (1lb 5oz) granulated sugar

100g (3½oz) unsalted butter

3 eggs

1 Simmer the blackberries and apple in enough water to cover in a pan, until soft. Sieve and put the juice in a double boiler.

2 Add the lemon juice, sugar and butter and stir over a low heat until the sugar dissolves. Beat the eggs and stir these into the blackberry mixture.

3 Cook gently until the mixture thickens. Pot in warm, sterilised jars and store in the fridge. Eat within 6 weeks.

This is a good way of using wild blackberries

Marrow, Tomato and Date Chutney

Ingredients

1.4kg (3lb) marrow

85g (3oz) salt

900g (2lb) red tomatoes, skinned and chopped

225g (8oz) onions, chopped

340g (12oz) cooking apples, peeled, cored and sliced

565ml (1 pint) distilled malt vinegar

225g (8oz) cooking dates, stoned and chopped

450g (1lb) soft light brown sugar

1 tablespoon mustard seeds

2 tablespoons ground ginger

2 teaspoons ground allspice

Making jams and pickles was an essential part of country life. There was always someone with a glut of fruit or vegetables, so even if individuals lacked their own gardens or orchards, the chances were that one of their neighbours would have some pears, apples, tomatoes or vegetable marrows to give away. This Devonshire recipe is good for using up gluts and the delicious chutney is excellent with beefburgers.

1 Peel the marrow, then cut it in half and remove and discard the seeds. Dice the flesh into 1cm (½in) cubes and layer these in a bowl with the salt. Cover and leave for 24 hours.

2 The following day, rinse the salted marrow thoroughly under cold running water and drain well; set aside.

3 Put the tomatoes, onions and apples in a large preserving pan. Add the vinegar, stir well, then bring to the boil. Reduce the heat and cook gently for 30 minutes. Add the dates, sugar and spices, followed by the marrow. Stir well and bring back to the boil. Reduce the heat and simmer for 1½–2 hours, until thick, stirring occasionally to prevent sticking. Pour into warm, sterilised jars, seal and store for 2–3 months before eating.

This recipe is good for using up gluts

Lallah's Chutney

Who Lallah was in real life is, sadly, unrecorded, but her delicious chutney recipe lives on. However, like most chutneys, it is better if left to mature for a few weeks before eating, so be patient and resist the temptation to tuck in immediately.

1 Pour the vinegar over the salt and sugar and then place in a large preserving pan with all the other ingredients.

2 Stir over a low heat until the sugar has completely dissolved, then simmer gently for about 3 hours, until the chutney thickens and the vegetables are tender.

3 Pour the hot mixture into warm, sterilised jars, then seal and store in the usual way for several weeks before eating.

Ingredients

500ml (18fl oz) malt vinegar

40g (1½oz) salt

250g (9oz) granulated sugar

1kg (2lb 3oz) large apples, peeled, cored and sliced

85g (3oz) preserved stem ginger in syrup, drained and sliced

55g (2oz) sultanas

30g (1oz) chillies, chopped

1 tablespoon mustard powder

1 shallot, chopped

1 medium onion, sliced

Mint Chutney

This is mint sauce with a difference – the chilli and vinegar combination is very good, especially after leaving for a few weeks to mellow.

1 Put the mint leaves, cider vinegar, sugar, garlic and chilli into a wide-mouthed jar, stirring well.

2 Cork and leave the jar on a sunny windowsill for 2 weeks, shaking the contents occasionally. It keeps well in the fridge. Serve the mint chutney with roast lamb.

Ingredients

50g (1¾oz) fresh mint leaves, finely chopped

150ml (¼ pint) cider vinegar

50g (1¾oz) granulated sugar

1 garlic clove, cut into slivers

1 green chilli, cut in half

Old-fashioned Red Tomato Chutney

Ingredients

1kg (2lb 3oz) tomatoes, skinned and cut in small chunks

140g (5oz) onions, chopped

300g (10½oz) apples, peeled, cored and chopped

300g (10½oz) granulated sugar

30g (1oz) salt

½ red chilli, deseeded and chopped

½ teaspoon English mustard powder

1 dessertspoon coriander seeds, crushed

8 allspice berries, crushed

345ml (12fl oz) malt vinegar

This is a spicy version of the much-loved classic red tomato chutney. It is a great accompaniment to cold meats and game, pies, and cheese and biscuits.

1 Mix all the ingredients together in a large preserving pan and place over a low heat, stirring gently until all the sugar has completely dissolved.

2 Simmer gently for about 2 hours, until the chutney is well reduced, thick and slightly brownish. Stir from time to time, more frequently towards the end of cooking, to make sure it doesn't stick to the pan and burn.

3 Remove the pan from the heat and pour the hot chutney into warm, sterilised jars and seal in the usual way. Store in a cool, dark place for a few weeks before eating.

Use really ripe red tomatoes for the best results

Pickled Pears

Eat this delicious and unusual preserve with cold meat. Pickled pears make good Christmas gifts.

1 Drop the prepared pears into a bowl of water with a good squeeze of lemon juice to prevent them browning.

2 Put the sugar, cloves and vinegar in a large preserving pan and stir well. Add the pears and bring to the boil. Cover and simmer very gently until tender. The timing depends on the pear variety; underripe Williams take about 1½ hours, but hard cooking pears may take much longer. Pot the pears and syrup in warm, sterilised jars and seal with parchment paper.

Ingredients

2kg (4½lb) hard pears, peeled, halved and cored (use underripe eating pears if no cooking pears are available)

lemon juice

1kg (2lb 3oz) sugar

3 cloves

200ml (7fl oz) distilled malt vinegar

Damson Pickle

A common use for damsons in the Lake District is to pickle them for eating with cheese or cold mutton.

1 Prick the damsons all over with a darning needle and put them in a bowl. Boil the vinegar, sugar and spices together and pour over the fruit. Cover and leave overnight.

2 The following day, drain and reserve the liquid and re-boil. Pour over the fruit again, then cover and leave for a second night. Repeat this process again the next day.

3 On the final day, boil the fruit and the liquid gently for about 5 minutes, trying not to let the skins break. Pot the damson pickle in warm, sterilised jars, then seal and keep for at least a month before eating, preferably longer.

Ingredients

700g (1lb 9oz) damsons, washed and dried

565ml (1 pint) vinegar (malt or distilled malt)

340g (12oz) granulated sugar

2–3 cloves

1 small stick of cinnamon

1 blade of mace

Sauces, Pastry and Stuffings

Salad Cream

Ingredients

2 eggs

¼ teaspoon salt

a pinch of sugar

a small pinch of cayenne pepper

a pinch of mustard powder

1 teaspoon water

150ml (¼ pint) double cream

*approximately 1 tablespoon
wine vinegar*

*approximately 1 tablespoon
tarragon or basil vinegar,
or other flavoured vinegar,
to taste*

SERVES 6 **English cookery tradition includes a distinctive type of salad dressing that is based on cream and cooked egg yolk. Some versions also include smoothly puréed, cooked potato as well. This recipe is based on one given by Eliza Acton in her *Modern Cookery for Private Families* (1845).**

1 Put the eggs in a saucepan of cold water, bring to the boil over a medium heat, then lower the heat and leave to simmer for 10 minutes. Remove the eggs and allow to cool.

2 Shell the eggs, remove the whites and put the yolks in a bowl or mortar. Use a wooden spoon or pestle to reduce the yolks to a paste, then stir in the salt, sugar, cayenne pepper, mustard and water. Add the cream, a tablespoon at a time, stirring well to make sure that the mixture is smooth. Once all the cream is incorporated, add the vinegars, taste the mixture and add extra seasoning or vinegar if necessary.

3 Alternatively, you can mix all the ingredients, except the cream and vinegars, to a paste in a blender. Then, while the blender is still running, pour in the cream and continue to blend until it is all just incorporated. Don't overblend or the cream will start to thicken. Quickly blend in the vinegars, taste and, as above, add any extra vinegar plus more seasoning if needed.

Red Onion Marmalade

 This is a simple take on a modern classic, to eat warm with plain roast duck, pork or goose.

1 Melt the butter in a small heavy frying pan over a low heat. Add the onion, cover the pan and cook very gently for about 30 minutes, stirring occasionally. The onion slices should become soft and translucent, but not brown.

2 Add the sherry and let it bubble a moment, then add the vinegar and star anise and bring the mixture to the boil. Stir in the sugar, season with a little salt and pepper and simmer gently, stirring frequently, for another 15–20 minutes, or until it has achieved the consistency of runny jam. Remove the star anise before serving.

Ingredients

30g (1oz) unsalted butter

1 red onion, cut in half and thinly sliced

1 tablespoon sweet sherry

2 tablespoons red wine vinegar

1 whole star anise

20g (¾oz) light soft brown sugar

salt and pepper

A simple take on a modern classic relish

Watercress Sauce for Salmon or Trout

Ingredients

1 bunch of watercress

300ml (½ pint) water or fish stock

30g (1oz) butter

30g (1oz) plain flour

1 tablespoon double cream

salt and pepper

squeeze of lemon juice

SERVES 4-6 **Layers of chalk and clay in a landscape, such as in Dorset and Hampshire, give springs of pure water, and clean water is the best environment for growing peppery watercress. If you're lucky, it also means good streams for trout fishing.**

1 Strip the leaves from the watercress and reserve. Chop the stalks and cook gently in the water or stock until just soft.

2 Melt the butter in a small pan over a low heat. Stir in the flour and cook for 1 minute without browning. Strain in the cooking liquid (discard the stalks) and cook gently, stirring constantly, until the sauce thickens. Stir in the cream and season to taste with salt and pepper. Add the lemon juice.

3 Finally, add the reserved watercress leaves to the sauce and serve immediately with fish, such as poached salmon, sea trout or river trout, or with eggs.

The perfect accompaniment for poached salmon

Onion Sauce

SERVES 4-6 **This sauce is the traditional accompaniment for hot salt duck, roast lamb or mutton.**

1 Put the onions and milk in a pan with a little of the butter and cook very gently until the onions are almost a purée.

2 In a separate pan, melt the rest of the butter and add the flour. Stir in the onion purée and bring to the boil. Season, adding a dusting of sugar if the onions seem to lack sweetness, and stir in the cream. Serve hot.

Ingredients

2 large onions, sliced

150ml (¼ pint) milk

30g (1oz) butter

1 tablespoon plain flour

salt, pepper and a little sugar

2–3 tablespoons double cream

Apple Sauce

SERVES 4-6 **Apple sauce is the ideal partner for roast pork and goose. It is very simple to make, so there's no need to buy a jar of ready-made sauce – and the home-made version tastes so superior.**

1 Cook the apples gently in a small saucepan with just enough water to prevent them from sticking over a very low heat. Stir frequently.

2 Once the apples have softened and become a purée, add about 3 teaspoons sugar, or to taste. If wished, stir in a small knob of butter.

Ingredients

2 large Bramley apples, peeled, cored and cut in chunks

3 teaspoons sugar

knob of butter (optional)

Orange Sauce

SERVES 2 **This is usually served with wild duck, and the bitter-sour flavour of Seville orange is better with this close-textured, gamey meat than sweet oranges, and makes a good midwinter combination. If you have to use sweet oranges, add a little bitter orange marmalade at the end.**

1 Melt the butter in a small pan and add the orange zest, cayenne pepper and lemon juice. Bring to the boil and cook for a minute to reduce slightly.

2 Taste, then add a pinch of salt and a little sugar until the bitter/sweet balance of the sauce is pleasing.

Ingredients

30g (1oz) unsalted butter

zest of 1 Seville orange, cut in fine strips and blanched in boiling water

a pinch of cayenne pepper

juice of 1 lemon

salt

sugar

Bread Sauce

SERVES 4 **Bread sauce is perfect with roast poultry and game birds. Recipes vary in their flavourings – nutmeg, cloves and mace appear in some, whereas onions are more usual than shallots. Be guided by your personal taste and family tradition.**

1 Put the milk in the top half of a double boiler or a bowl over simmering water. Stick the cloves into the shallots, add to the milk and infuse for about 1 hour. Strain, discarding the shallots.

2 Return the flavoured milk to the pan or bowl and stir in the breadcrumbs. Place over hot water again for about 10–15 minutes, during which the sauce should thicken up (not too much – if necessary add a little hot milk). Taste and add a little salt and pepper. Stir in the cream and serve.

Ingredients

300ml (½ pint) full-cream milk

2 cloves

85g (3oz) shallots, peeled

85g (3oz) fine breadcrumbs made from slightly stale white bread

salt and pepper

3 tablespoons single cream

Cumberland Sauce

Ingredients

zest of 1 orange (preferably unwaxed), cut in thin strips

zest of 1 lemon (preferably unwaxed), cut in thin strips

4 tablespoons redcurrant jelly

4 tablespoons port

1 teaspoon smooth Dijon mustard

a pinch of ground ginger

SERVES 4-6 **A delicious sauce for cold ham or game, this appears to have no links with the county of that name, and a legend associating it with the royal title of the Duke of Cumberland seems to be just that – a legend. The base of redcurrant jelly and wine is reminiscent of eighteenth-century sauces for venison, but the first recognisable recipe was given (under a different name) by Alexis Soyer in 1853. It seems to have been the French chef Georges Auguste Escoffier who popularised the recipe and made it a commercial success in the nineteenth century.**

1 Put the strips of orange and lemon zest in a small bowl, then cover them with boiling water and leave to blanch for about 3–4 minutes. Drain well.

2 Melt the redcurrant jelly in a small pan, stirring gently to smooth out any lumps. Add the port and mix well. Stir in the drained orange and lemon zest, the mustard and a little ginger. Taste and add a little more mustard or ginger if desired.

3 Allow to cool before serving the Cumberland sauce with cold meat. It goes particularly well with gammon, ham, game birds and coarse pâtés and terrines.

*A delicious sauce
for cold ham or game*

Shortcrust Pastry

Ingredients

*310g (11oz) plain flour mixed
with a generous pinch of salt*

*140g (5oz) lard, butter, or lard
and butter mixed*

6–8 tablespoons cold water

**Shortcrust pastry is very simple to make. You can use
lard for a very short pastry or butter for good
flavour – or a mixture of the two. Solid vegetable fat
and margarine can both be used for pastry making,
but reduced fat and low-fat spreads are unsuitable.**

1 Put the flour and salt in a large mixing bowl. Cut the fat into
1cm (½in) dice and add to the bowl. Using just the tips of
your fingers, lightly rub the fat into the flour until the mixture
resembles fine breadcrumbs.

2 Now add enough cold water, a little at a time, to make a
coherent dough – a little less or a little more may be needed,
depending on how dry the flour is.

3 Shape the dough into a ball, then wrap it in foil and put in
the refrigerator or a cool place for at least 30 minutes to rest
before using. This makes 450g (1lb) pastry.

*Shortcrust pastry
is very simple to make*

Puff Pastry

Ingredients

*250g (9oz) plain flour, plus extra
for working and rolling*

about ½ teaspoon salt

*170g (6oz) chilled fat (equal
quantities of butter and lard)*

iced water

This recipe is a simplified version of the fine French puff pastry and is known in British cookery as 'rough puff pastry'. It won't rise as much as true puff pastry, but is still good. Alternatively, you can find ready-made pastry in the chill cabinets of supermarket freezers, either as blocks or ready-rolled sheets. This makes the cook's life much easier. When making puff pastry, the fat must be cold from the fridge. Use a sharp knife to cut the pastry, and don't crush the cut edges or get egg wash on them, or it won't rise well.

1 Put the flour in a large bowl and add thn salt. Use the coarse side of a grater to grate the butter and lard into the flour (dipping the fat into the flour periodically makes this easier). Once all the fat is in, start adding iced water, a tablespoon at a time, stirring with your hand until a stiff paste forms. Don't overdo the water – the mixture must be coherent but not sticky.

2 Turn the dough on to a floured work surface and work for a moment, just enough to make sure the mixture is even. Then roll out into an oblong three times as long as it is wide; turn the top third down towards you and the bottom third up to cover this. Turn 90 degrees clockwise and repeat the rolling and folding process, then chill for 30 minutes.

3 Repeat this rolling and folding process twice more, then give the pastry a final rest and it is ready for use. It can be made a day in advance; if you do this, wrap it in foil or clingfilm and store in the fridge overnight.

*The fat must be cold
from the fridge*

Dumplings

SERVES 4 **Suet dumplings are comforting companions for a meaty stew, particularly one made with beef. They probably share a common ancestor with suet puddings, and are rib-sticking food intended to stretch precious supplies of other, more expensive ingredients. They are simple to make and easy to vary with different flavourings. Make the mixture just before you want to cook it. Plain flour mixed with 1 teaspoon baking powder can be used instead of self-raising flour if desired. The stew they are destined for needs to be completely cooked. Bear in mind that the dumplings will need about 25 minutes to cook after they have been added.**

1 Put all the dry ingredients in a large bowl. Add the flavouring ingredients if desired. Then add about two-thirds of the water and mix. The mixture should be fairly soft but not too sticky. Add a little more water if it seems dry. Form the mixture into balls the size of a large walnut and drop them on top of the stew.

2 If the stew is cooking in the oven, leave it uncovered after adding the dumplings. They will crisp slightly on top, and may colour a little in the heat. If the stew is cooking on the hob, drop the dumplings into the liquid and cover the pan.

3 Cook for a further 20–30 minutes in a preheated moderate oven at 180°C, 350°F, Gas mark 4 until the dumplings are cooked through and slightly golden on top. Alternatively, allow about 20 minutes for a stew cooking on the hob.

Ingredients

115g (4oz) self-raising flour

60g (2¼oz) shredded suet

a pinch of salt

about 120ml (4fl oz) water

Flavourings

1 generous tablespoon chopped fresh parsley with a little thyme and marjoram; or 1 generous teaspoon mustard powder and about 1 tablespoon chopped fresh parsley or chives; or 1 generous tablespoon creamed horseradish; or a little chopped fresh tarragon

Caramelised Apples

Ingredients

30g (1oz) unsalted butter

*3 large apples, such as Cox's or
a dryish, aromatic eating apple,
peeled, cored and sliced,
but not too thinly*

1 whole star anise (optional)

1 dessertspoon cider vinegar

2 tablespoons sugar

SERVES 4-6 **These savoury caramelised apples are very good served with roast pork, goose or duck, and make an unusual and pleasant change from the traditional apple sauce. If serving them with duck, try adding a little grated orange zest at the end. The apples must be a firm-fleshed type that will keep their shape and not collapse when cooked.**

1 Melt the butter in a heavy frying pan and add the apple slices, and the star anise, if using. Cook gently over a very low heat, stirring frequently, until the apple is starting to soften and has become slightly translucent.

2 Add the cider vinegar, then stir in the sugar and continue to cook until the apple begins to caramelise. However, take care not to let it get too brown and burn. Serve tepid.

*The apples must
be a firm-fleshed type*

Potato and Apple Stuffing

Ingredients

85g (3oz) unsalted butter

1 large onion, chopped

*600g (1lb 5oz) floury potatoes,
cut into chunks*

2 garlic cloves, crushed

salt

1 tablespoon chopped fresh sage

*2 large apples, such as Cox's or
a dryish, aromatic eating apple,
peeled, cored and cut into chunks*

pepper

**Mashed potatoes are excellent for stuffing goose.
Alexis Soyer advocated them in the mid-nineteenth
century, in combination with apples, although the
idea of using them didn't really become popular in
English cookery until the middle of the last century.**

1 Melt the butter in a large frying pan over a low heat, then
add the onion and cook very gently until it softens and
begins to turn golden brown.

2 Boil the potatoes in a large pan of salted water, then drain
and mash. Stir in the cooked onions, the garlic, sage, a
generous teaspoon of salt and a generous seasoning of pepper.
Mix the pieces of apple through the mixture and use it to stuff
a 5–7kg (11–15lb) goose.

Mashed potatoes are excellent
for stuffing goose

Dried Apricot and Almond Stuffing

While lamb or mutton cooked on the bone scores best for flavour, it is not the easiest thing to carve. Both leg and shoulder joints are often boned to create joints that are ideal for stuffing. This recipe uses a fruit and nut combination, which is derived from Arab cookery. Use it to stuff a joint, or make into delicious little stuffing balls for roasting.

1 Melt the butter in a small frying pan and sauté the onion gently until translucent. Toast the almonds lightly in the oven for 5–10 minutes; watch to make sure they don't burn.

2 In a bowl, combine the onion, almonds, bread, apricots and lemon zest. Season with a generous grating of nutmeg, the salt and some pepper. Mix well and pour in just enough stock or milk to make the bread moist but not soggy.

3 Use to stuff the cavity left by boning a medium shoulder of lamb or leg of lamb. Alternatively, form into small balls and bake in a lightly greased dish for about 20–30 minutes in a preheated moderate oven at 180°C, 350°F, Gas mark 4.

Ingredients

40g (1½oz) unsalted butter

1 small onion, finely chopped

55g (2oz) almonds, blanched and cut into slivers

140g (5oz) crustless day-old white bread, torn into small pieces

85g (3oz) dried apricots, soaked for a few hours, then drained and roughly chopped

zest of ½ lemon (preferably unwaxed), finely grated

a pinch of grated nutmeg

½ teaspoon salt

pepper

55–100ml (2–3½fl oz) stock or milk

Sage and Onion Stuffing

Ingredients

1 large onion, peeled

12 fresh sage leaves

60g (2½oz) stale breadcrumbs

*20g (¾oz) unsalted butter,
cut in small pieces (or beef suet
for a traditional mixture)*

1 egg, beaten

½ teaspoon salt

pepper

This recipe, which is suitable for pork, goose or duck, was considered old-fashioned by the 1840s. It was also thought too overpowering by Victorian cooks, although Eliza Acton remarked that some people always liked it with leg of pork (which was stuffed at the knuckle end). However, it has outlived the Victorians and it remains one of the most iconic stuffing mixtures in the English kitchen.

1 Put the onion in a saucepan, cover with boiling water and simmer for 20–30 minutes, or until tender. Drain. Once it is cool enough to handle, cut it into quarters. Put it in a food processor with the sage and chop (but don't reduce it to a purée), or chop together by hand until fairly fine.

2 Transfer the onion and sage mixture to a bowl and stir in the breadcrumbs, butter and enough egg to bind lightly, then stir in the seasoning (don't use the processor, which makes the mixture too runny).

3 Use this stuffing mixture to stuff a boned and rolled pork roast or a bird, or press into a greased dish and bake along with the roast for the last 30 minutes of cooking time.

Chestnut and Prune Stuffing

Chestnut stuffing is more commonly associated with Christmas turkey, but it can also be very good with goose. The same is true for prunes, which are quite often used with goose in continental Europe. Like potato stuffing, this didn't make much of an impact in British cookery until the mid-twentieth century.

Ingredients

15g (½oz) unsalted butter

1–2 shallots, finely chopped

1 garlic clove, crushed

200–250g (7–9oz) chestnut purée

200–250g (7–9oz) sausage meat

pepper

about 12 prunes (ready-to-eat, or soaked dried ones), pitted

2 large apples, such as Cox's or a dryish, aromatic eating apple, peeled, cored and sliced

1 scant teaspoon salt

1 Melt the butter in a small pan over a low heat and fry the shallots and garlic lightly, until softened.

2 Put the chestnut purée in a bowl and break it up. Mix in the fried shallots and garlic, the sausage meat, salt and a generous seasoning of black pepper.

3 Put half this stuffing mixture into a 5–7kg (11–15lb) goose, then add the prunes and apples in a layer, and spread the remainder of the stuffing over them.

Chestnut stuffing is very good with goose

Fried Breadcrumbs

 A classic British accompaniment for game, in use since at least the nineteenth century.

Ingredients

15g (½oz) unsalted butter

55g (2oz) breadcrumbs, made from stale white bread

Melt the butter in a small frying pan. Don't let it burn. Add the breadcrumbs and fry gently, stirring frequently, for 5–10 minutes, or until the crumbs are crisp and golden.

Game Chips

It is difficult to recommend how many potatoes to use, as people will eat as many game chips as put in front of them, or until you get fed up with frying.

Ingredients

Maris Piper potatoes, peeled

oil or beef dripping, for deep-fat frying

salt

1 Cut the potatoes into very narrow strips, about 2mm (¹⁄₁₆in) thick and the same wide, and as long as the potatoes allow. Drop into a bowl of cold water and leave for about 15 minutes.

2 When you are ready to cook, drain them and spread out on a cloth or kitchen paper and dry them thoroughly (this is important, otherwise they will make the hot oil spit viciously).

3 Heat the oil or fat in a deep-fat fryer. The recommended temperature is 180–185°C, 350–360°F. Alternatively, drop a small cube of bread into the hot fat and observe how long it takes to brown; if it rises to the surface and browns in 30 seconds, it is hot enough (don't let it get to smoking point).

4 When the fat is hot enough, fry the chips in batches – don't overcrowd the pan. Cook briskly until golden, then remove with a slotted spoon and drain well on kitchen paper. Sprinkle with salt – a flaky one such as Maldon looks nice – and serve.

Forcemeat Balls and Butterballs

Ingredients

115g (4oz) fresh breadcrumbs

60g (2¼oz) butter

1 egg yolk

grated zest of 2 large lemons

3 tablespoons chopped fresh parsley

1 tablespoon chopped fresh thyme leaves

a generous grating of nutmeg

1 teaspoon salt

pepper

butter, for frying

SERVES 4

Forcemeat balls are considerably more elegant than dumplings. They are a traditional garnish for game dishes and were also added to pie fillings. In the past they were usually fried, but they can be cooked in the oven if preferred. Forcemeat balls can also be made very small. 'Butterballs' are essentially forcemeat balls made without flavourings.

1 To make the forcemeat, put all the ingredients except the butter in the goblet of a processor or blender. Process for a few seconds to give a smooth paste. Shape this into walnut-sized balls and fry them gently in butter, turning frequently, for about 10 minutes. Add them to a stew before serving.

2 Alternatively, put the forcemeat balls in a greased baking dish and bake in a preheated moderate oven at 180°C, 350°F, Gas mark 4 for 20 minutes.

3 For butterballs, use only the breadcrumbs, butter, egg yolk and a pinch of salt. Make them very small – about the size of hazelnuts – and poach gently in a stew for 5–10 minutes. They are excellent with delicate fish or vegetable stews.

Index

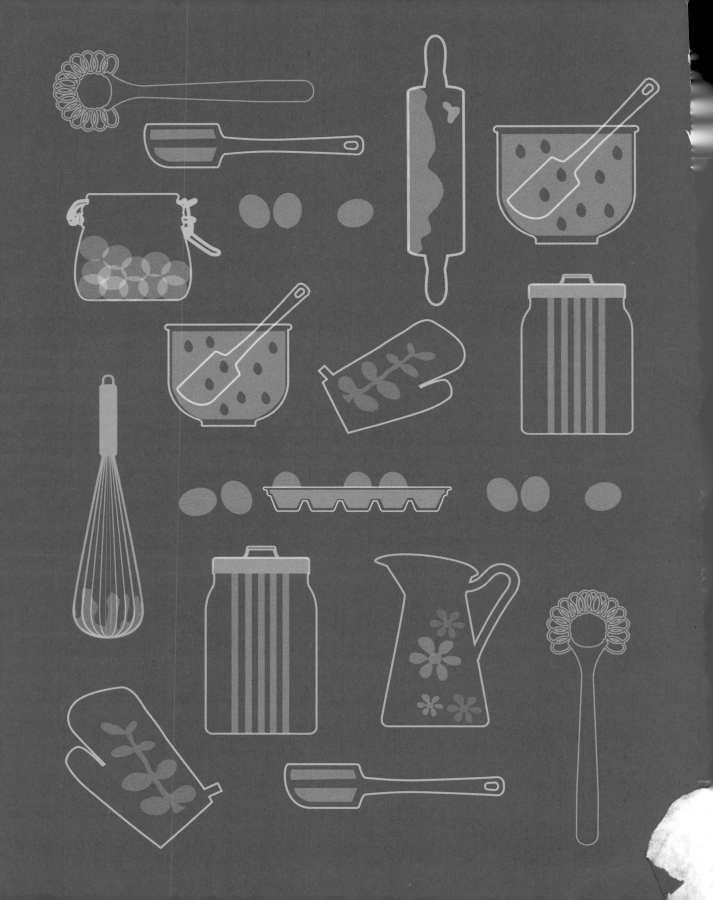